Heaven's Wait

An inspiring journey of love, healing and
transformation; from overcoming an introduction
to spirituality based on fear to receiving loving
guidance and intuitive messages from spirit!

PAULA SEVESTRE

BALBOA
PRESS
A DIVISION OF HAY HOUSE

Copyright © 2014 Paula Sevestre.

All rights reserved. No part of this book may be used or reproduced by any means, graphic, electronic, or mechanical, including photocopying, recording, taping or by any information storage retrieval system without the written permission of the publisher except in the case of brief quotations embodied in critical articles and reviews.

Balboa Press books may be ordered through booksellers or by contacting:

Balboa Press
A Division of Hay House
1663 Liberty Drive
Bloomington, IN 47403
www.balboapress.com
1 (877) 407-4847

Because of the dynamic nature of the Internet, any web addresses or links contained in this book may have changed since publication and may no longer be valid. The views expressed in this work are solely those of the author and do not necessarily reflect the views of the publisher, and the publisher hereby disclaims any responsibility for them.

The author of this book does not dispense medical advice or prescribe the use of any technique as a form of treatment for physical, emotional, or medical problems without the advice of a physician, either directly or indirectly. The intent of the author is only to offer information of a general nature to help you in your quest for emotional and spiritual well-being. In the event you use any of the information in this book for yourself, which is your constitutional right, the author and the publisher assume no responsibility for your actions.

Any people depicted in stock imagery provided by Thinkstock are models, and such images are being used for illustrative purposes only.
Certain stock imagery © Thinkstock.

Printed in the United States of America.

ISBN: 978-1-4525-1793-3 (sc)
ISBN: 978-1-4525-1795-7 (hc)
ISBN: 978-1-4525-1794-0 (e)

Library of Congress Control Number: 2014912098

Balboa Press rev. date: 07/18/2014

Dedication 1

To Mark, my husband,
Whose love and strength never wavered!

To Nathaniel and Bradley, my twin boys,
Who trusted that we were doing what was best for them!

To my family,
Whose love, care, and support know no bounds!

To my friend Dawn, and her girls Emma and Cassie,
Whose friendship comforted in our time of need!

Dedication 2

In loving memory
Of my parents,
Bernie and Ruth,
And my brother,
Bradley,
Whose love endures and inspires in spirit as in life.

Preface

I don't know when it started, but early in my life, I was able to project what other people saw in me. This would have both negative and positive implications. I didn't realize it at the time, but this would shape my entire life. It wasn't easy. If anything it was tiring always molding and shaping the person inside me. I was always told I got along well with others and that I communicated effectively; however, much of that communication was one way. I sensed what would make an individual responsive to me, and I became that person.

Manipulation is an art form. It can be used for both good and bad. If you are equally challenged to overcome this lesson in your lifetime, it is much more exaggerated. You will be presented lesson after lesson until you recognize that which you have come to this earth plane to learn. Only then will you be able to take the necessary steps to lessen the effects on your life. It becomes important to understand your life's purpose and seek ways in which to rein in the negative aspects of that life lesson—to begin to build upon only that which is positive to prevent further lessons from creating obstacles to your development.

Introduction

It was Tuesday, April 15, 2014, and I was standing at the kitchen sink washing up the breakfast dishes. My mind was lost in thought with the upcoming long-awaited family vacation, which included my friend and her two girls. It was three weeks away. What made the wait even more difficult was the snow that developed during the night. Spring was put on the back burner for this day. I could sense the energy around me, guiding through my hair. I was trying to shake it off until I finished my housework, but they were insistent. Finally there was a thunderous boom in the house, almost like a summer's rainstorm. I opened the kitchen door and asked my husband, who was changing his tire, if he heard the sound too. He didn't—not a thing. I closed the door and pondered whether the noise could have been something else. In my heart I knew it wasn't ... I thought, *I had better meditate.*

My name is Paula Sevestre. I was born on a small First Nation community in Cape Breton, Nova Scotia. For those unfamiliar with the term *First Nation*, it is reserve land that has been set aside by the federal government of Canada for the exclusive use of registered Indians in Canada. There are 634 First Nations in Canada consisting of many different nations and tribes. I am Mi'kmaq. I have been married to my husband, Mark, for twenty years, and have twin boys Nathaniel and Bradley. We currently reside in southern Ontario. My husband is Mohawk.

I would be turning fifty soon, and that was the reason for our upcoming family vacation. My spiritual journey began three years earlier, and we had not traveled for leisure in that three-year time period. I had traveled to Cape Breton to assist with my ailing mother's care but not travel that would be considered vacation travel. All this was set aside as I made my way through an often-challenging spiritual journey. I am currently a consultant, and I have completed contract work of varying degrees over the past fifteen years. I work hard and enjoy research. I credit this love of research for saving my life, my very existence, from something that could have destroyed my life, my marriage, and my belief in God.

Chapter 1

I was raised Catholic but floated in and out of regular practice. I was continually struck by the notion of time. I would see others around me checking the time; is it time to leave, time to get on with my day, time to have a drink, time to eat, time to get out! Unfortunately, I understood this because I was that way too. I wanted to believe I was spiritual, I was one with God, but it had a time limit. I didn't want it to interrupt my life; I had important things to do!

Then, seemingly out of the blue, on November 22, 2010, time seemed to stand still. There was no big accident, no big, life-altering event, just manipulation coming back to take a great big chunk out of my backside. When they say, "What goes around comes around," you better believe it!

I went to work like any other Monday morning. We had a few beers the day before, so I was feeling tired, but I had a full schedule that day and got straight to work. I was planning to host some workshops later that month, and I still had a lot of tasks to complete. I really didn't feel like socializing and stayed in my office to eat my lunch. However, I was called to join someone else; reluctantly I went. That was the day I encountered an individual who called himself a traditional healer. He had a message for me.

Aboriginal traditional healers were not common in the community in which I was raised; the only thing I knew about traditional healers is what I may have read in books. I may have been aware of some medicine people in our nation, but we were firmly entrenched in Western medicine and the Christian faith. So I was definitely unnerved when this person said that he had a message for me—especially from someone I thought had supernatural powers!

My own family members have experienced spiritual happenings, so I was not unfamiliar with the concept of the spiritual realm, including visions, apparitions, and communications with spirit, but that was them, not me!

This healer was my age. His message was that if I went home to see my mother in December, my family would not let me leave because they did not want the responsibility of looking after her. He said my siblings would abandon me and I would be forced to stay there and would eventually be driven to a mental breakdown from which I would never recover.

This sounds crazy, right? Because it is crazy!

My family is very loving, and there was no reason whatsoever to believe any of this, but I did! I asked him what I could do to prevent this from happening. He said I would need to come for a reading at his place. We scheduled one for 5:00 p.m. that evening. He said it was urgent. I remember the day like it was just happening.

I arrived at his little place behind his homestead. It was raining. I was feeling a little nervous, but I made sure to let my husband know where I was going. The one twelve-by-twelve room was small and smoky, with the smell of white sage. There was one window open, but it was still very dense with smoke. I went in and sat down. There were only two chairs at the small table. He asked me if I was there out of my own free will. I said yes. He asked me to put my hand in some tobacco and hold it for a few seconds. He then touched the tobacco where I had held it and began to communicate with someone he said was my spirit guide.

He said my spirit guide was very upset with me and that it had been trying to get my attention for a long time but that I would not listen. I began to shake at this time. He said that I had a lot to make up for and that I would need to change my life—that I would not even look like the same person when I was finished with this work. He said that I looked like a clown with the makeup I wore and that my hair should not have the blond highlights that it currently had. He said the spirit guide showed him an image of when I was a child, and I looked nothing like I should look as a native person. (I am considered attractive and I wore the proper amount of makeup and highlighted my hair, but in no way did I think this would be a concern to my guide.)

He then said I had lived my life for myself long enough and that my boys, who were seven at the time, needed to learn their path in the traditional way. They would need to learn how to survive without modern conveniences and understand plants and medicines. I too would need to learn plants and traditional medicine and ceremonies. I was to reinvent myself into a person people could easily connect with and not have my image getting in the way. I would walk this earth in moccasins, close to Mother Earth.

He said if I didn't change my ways that he saw my death; I would be full of cancer. It would be in places around my body that he said I used to manipulate people but first I would be viciously gang raped by people who were watching me. It would be so savage that they would leave my face beaten to a point that I would be unrecognizable.

In this time too, I was directed to quit drinking. It had to be my free will to do so. I had to make a promise to the Creator that I would quit drinking. I was told to go home and empty any remaining alcohol into the earth at the end of my property. I was not to have any alcohol cross my doorway again. At this time I lived in the city of Brantford, Ontario. He also suggested that negative spirits were around me and my family and that we would need to protect ourselves. This scared me in ways one can only imagine. Images from movies like *The Exorcist*, *The Shining*, and *The Amityville Horror* filled my head. By the time I got home, I was beginning to feel afraid of the dark.

The first reading went on for over an hour. It rained hard the entire time. I got home and emptied all the alcohol that was in the house. I told my husband what had happened and that I was going to quit drinking. My husband was not so sure of the whole thing and did not want me to make any snap decisions. He didn't feel we drank in an out-of-control manner or that we neglected our sons in any way. We were quite happy and lived our lives quietly. We were both in our forties and had children late in our lives, so we were both very content with being homebodies. We were both busy and enjoyed our work.

I think, too, that things would have remained the same was it not for another message I had to see the healer; it was urgent, and it involved my husband. My husband had just left for a trip to Ottawa that day. I was still thinking about the reading, but it didn't have as much impact on me, and I was not as frightened as when I first met with the healer. I was willing to let it go—to continue on with my life.

I went to see the healer again after work; I was frightened beyond belief. I sat down, and he asked for my wedding ring. I gave it to him, and he held it while he did the reading.

He said that he was shown a vision of how Mark, my husband, would die. He said that if Mark prevented me from taking the steps necessary for my healing, that spirit would not allow him to stand in my way. He could not interfere with my path. He would be in a car crash with some friends, and he would not be found for a long period of time. In that time, he would suffer terribly before he died. He said that something sharp would pierce Mark's chest during the car accident, and it would be a while before he died. He would be calling out to the Creator for help, and he would be made to see the error in his ways. I started crying. How could I stop this? I didn't care about my own damnation, but Mark didn't harm anyone!

I was told that I would need to commit to a year's healing and that it involved a tremendous amount of work from both me and my husband. It was my responsibility to bring my husband on board with the healing process. We had to walk this journey together but could not interfere with the other's path. It would be easier for us if we were both committed to the healing process. Mark could not drink any alcohol, especially in our home. We had to sacrifice to save our own lives and the future of our children. The healing process had to start immediately. I left the small cabin and drove home in tears.

I called Mark and asked him to come home; he would need to leave his meeting early. He said he would be home as soon as possible and promised not to have any alcohol at the event in Ottawa. When he arrived home, I was prepared with my argument. I was ready to convince him to start the healing journey with me. We lay in bed together as I walked him through the reading. He was shocked. You have to understand that Mark is very pragmatic. This did not make sense to him, and it was a lot to absorb. However, I was insistent that we not put our kids in any jeopardy and that he had to know I would move forward on this healing journey alone if it meant that the he and the boys would be safe. I couldn't allow him or the boys to suffer any punishment because of my sins. He reluctantly agreed to a reading with the healer.

I basically forced his hand. If Mark didn't go to the healer, our marriage would be over. I was willing to destroy our family because of fear. Everything I put trust in was turned upside down. I didn't have a strong foothold on any one spiritual path, so I was easily influenced. I was so frightened at this time that I was scared to even take the garbage out to the bins in the laneway. I was scared of the dark, of negative spirits and entities that could invade our home. I was told that demons were everywhere and that I had to be prepared to encounter them when the time was right. If there was any fear in me, they would take advantage of this fact. I was told of all the people who used bad medicine in the community to win at gambling, sports, and competitions, to get lovers, for vindication, and the list goes on. But he was good. His duty was to help people afflicted by bad medicine and negative spirits. Everything the healer directed me to do, I did.

That first week was surreal. I tried to do my work and not think about everything. I didn't have my usual support because the healer warned me against talking to anyone about the healing process. I had Mark, but I couldn't express any doubts with him as it would weaken his reluctant acceptance to move forward with the healing. I began to feel awkward with the way I looked. I dyed my hair to its normal color of brown. I didn't want to dress in my usual business manner. I slowly started eliminating makeup from my morning routine. I didn't trust anyone at work because I was told by the healer that a few people at work used bad medicine and to watch out for them. I was also to buy a dream book and start recording my dreams to share with the healer who had the same dream book. (In hindsight, this was not a good idea as all of the dreams I reported were shaped by his interpretation. I did not trust my own.)

My best friend didn't know what hit her. All of a sudden she had these friends who were changing before her eyes. She didn't know if we could still be friends with her and if that was acceptable in our new traditional life. She was not an Aboriginal; I actually asked the healer if that should be a consideration. I note this because the healer had some very biased views about non-natives. On one hand he would say that we are all equal, but then he would say that he couldn't wait to see white people suffer when events unfolded in the future—events that would mark the end of the world as we know it.

Fortunately, we remained best friends. I could not have made a recovery without her.

We were directed to drink protection medicine that the healer prepared. Our entire family drank this each morning for the first month. In addition, I was asked to drink herbal tea that was meant to cleanse my body. It tasted like dandelions. I was asked to smudge our house to protect it from negative spirits. Mark was given another protection medicine that he was to sprinkle throughout the base of our entire house.

This was just the beginning of the payments to the healer for various protection medicines or teas that he prepared for me, Mark, or our family. Each time this cost could be anywhere from $40 to $120, depending on the stated need. In addition, each reading was another payment. The healer would determine when a reading was needed. This could be once or twice a week for each of us depending on the messages he got from his spirit guides. He required our cell numbers so he could text us instructions. We both grew to hate the sound of our cell phones' text message indicator.

That first week also marked the beginning of the release sessions. This was overnight work that came with a hefty price tag. It was $900 for my first release session. It was $1,100 for my husband's. This was startling. I remember getting the amount texted to me, and I didn't know how I would tell Mark. The healer's response was that we had to pay because of our arrogance and our way of life. He said our spirit guides said we were going to have to pay big time! I truly believe the healer thought we had more money than we actually did.

In preparation for my release work, the healer scheduled a three-day body cleanse session using red whip tea to induce vomiting. This was done for three consecutive mornings prior to the release session. It would usually last an hour and start at sunrise.

According to the healer, release work is examining every aspect of your life and letting it go to the Creator for healing. Situations that may have created fear, anger, resentment, jealousy, vindictiveness, or any type of negative feelings were to be remembered, examined, and let go in the morning with a pipe ceremony. The healer said these sessions were between me and the Creator. He said he had the ability to go elsewhere in spirit while I was doing the release work. (I thought to myself at this time, *Well then why do I need him!*) The memories were not to be brought up again once released. It had to start at my very earliest memory.

Chapter 2

I arrived at my first release session at 9:30 p.m. When I arrived the healer left the cabin so I could wash with a protection medicine that would protect me from negative spirits. The release work was to be done at night. The healer said this was the time when spirits would be most active; the spirit world is backward, and when we are asleep, they are awake. The spirit world would guide the sessions. A reading was then done to direct the healer on what was to be discussed in that first session. During this time the healer said the spirit guides said I was a very bad person and that it would take a long time for me to complete all the release sessions. I was immediately on edge.

I wanted to please the spirit guides by doing all the work and not feel tired throughout the night. I would only get a few short breaks from talking about my childhood for bathroom breaks. I had to drink three large jars of protection medicine throughout the night, so bathroom breaks were a necessity. There was only an outdoor toilet. The healer would warn of negative spirits outside the cabin, and he would stand guard while I went to the toilet. This scared me even more. I didn't like being in the dark outhouse. I couldn't wait to get back to the safety of the cabin, where at least I was not alone.

The healer opened the session with a pipe ceremony, and I was directed to go to my earliest childhood memory. The healer said he would go into a trance state while I spoke throughout the night. It took me a while to remember events in an age sequence like I was directed. They were jumbled, skipping all over my childhood, ten years old to six to eight. I was getting confused and nervous. I felt like I had to say something, anything!

I started. Our house was small and old. It had a wood stove and was heated by a coal furnace. There was a big heating vent in the middle of the hallway, and it had three bedrooms. There were nine children in total, five girls and four boys. I remember sleeping in a room with my sisters. There were two beds, one a double and the other a cot. I sucked my thumb. I remember my sister trying to pull my finger out of my mouth. I got earaches that were very painful. My mother used to heat an iron, unplug it, and place it near my face with a towel over it to help ease the pain of the earache. It seemed to work most times, and I was able to sleep.

We were a typical family that lived on the reserve. A few families were in better shape than ours, and some lived in worse conditions. We were definitely poor, but our door was always open and my parents welcomed many friends and relatives who traveled from other communities. Like many families on the reserve, alcohol and spousal abuse were common and had a significant impact on our entire family to one degree or another. However, there were many fun times that our family experienced. But I was not to remember those times, only times that created negative feelings or bad memories.

I was climbing around our kitchen sideboard. I always liked to look in the cupboards. My mother had just placed a pot of boiling water in the sink. Our water was heated in that manner as we didn't have hot water. I tried to step across the sink to the other side of the counter, but I slipped. I fell into the boiling water. My backside landed in the water. I don't remember crying, but I remember the ride to the hospital. A man who had a taxi service on the reserve drove us to the hospital, which was only a short distance from our home. I was just scalded. It was expected to heal, and the redness would go away in a short while. I don't think that stopped me from looking around in the cupboards. I always thought I might find money.

Usually when my father, who was a barber, got paid, we would get some pizza and pop on Saturday night. Sometimes we would also get an extra treat. I loved flakes. They were turnovers with jelly and cream inside and cost ten cents. My father was going to the store one Sunday, and I wanted a flake. I begged for one, but my parents couldn't afford it. Angry, I walked out the back door and down our steps. The kitchen window was located near the back steps, and as I descended the steps, I bust my hand though the window and cut my hand on the side of my palm. What possessed me to take that action, I don't know; it was just an impulse. I don't think I intended to break the window, but I did; it was covered in cardboard for quite some time.

We used to walk to the main road, Alexander Street, to catch the city bus to school. It was only a fifteen- or twenty-minute walk, but it seemed really far. It was just off the reserve. There was a little store called Leslie's where we would get off the bus. One day my brother had crossed the road in front of the bus, and a driver did not see him. He was struck, and his rubber boots flew off his feet. I remember seeing his boots and taking off home. I ran all the way home and told my mother that my brother had been hit; I'm sure my older siblings were with him. My mother didn't believe me right away; I had to convince her it was truth. I lied a lot when I was a kid. He was in the hospital for quite some time and got presents from the driver who hit him; I'm sure the driver felt terrible for what had happened. My brother made a full recovery.

We lived in this house up until I was five or six. I remember the day we had to move out. I was playing in the back bedroom, the boys' bedroom. They had two old army bunk beds in the room and a homemade clothes-storage unit. It was leaning against the back wall. It had been raining all day. Our house had always leaked, and there were buckets and pots all over to catch the rain leaking through the roof. I was playing in the boys' room and could see the ceiling drooping near the back wall above the storage unit. It had been leaking all day, but now it was raining so hard that the water was gathering in the ceiling. It was getting heavier and heavier. I remember looking at the sagging ceiling; it was starting to bulge. The whole back corner was starting to bulge. The water that accumulated in the ceiling crashed through and left half the ceiling hanging down. It was a disaster. I don't know the exact sequence of events that happened, but we had to move out of the house. We were going to move temporarily to a house where an older man had just passed away and the house was vacant.

We moved to the house using whatever means available to move our furniture, including toboggans and wagons. I'm sure my brothers were very busy going back and forth to collect our things and move them to the temporary house. I didn't mind moving, but when we got to the house, my mother pointed to the room in which the girls would sleep. I didn't want to sleep in that room. I remember attending the recent wake of the man who had just died, and our bed was being placed in the exact spot where his coffin was positioned. I had the spot against the wall. It was creepy! I don't know if I slept that entire first night.

It was and still is very common to host a wake for the recently deceased in our homes. The wakes are usually packed and are open to visitors around the clock for two nights and three days. The family, with the assistance of other community members, provides food and beverages to all visitors. Alcohol is not served at any of our wakes or post funeral dinners. A salite or auction is hosted as part of the post-funeral dinner. Items that are auctioned are donated by community members and may be offered as individual items or items that have been grouped together such as bedding, dishes, etc. Many items are brand new and are purchased by community members to donate to the salite. In most cases the funds raised during the salite are enough to cover the entire funeral expense for the deceased.

I guess I got used to the room and the creepy walk-up stairway to the attic that was located in the bedroom. I know we had rats. They were from the stream that was located near the end of the road. We had cats to help with the situation, but they could always be heard in the house. Our old house was being rebuilt using funds provided to our reserve for housing from the federal government. It took almost three years to build depending on funding availability.

We didn't have a telephone, so we relied on a neighbor across the street to assist in emergencies, and we had a lot. It was usually to call the police because my father was drinking and would beat up my mother. It wasn't that he just drank—they both did, and the situation easily got out of control. My father was usually so kind and gentle when sober but was the biggest asshole when drunk. One of us would usually run over to the neighbor's house in tears screaming to call the police. My brothers would do their best to get my father out of the house, but he would often try to get back inside. On one particular night, we were running from room to room trying to close the windows, but he caught my mother by the hair in the boys' bedroom as she leaned down to shut the window, and he dragged her right out the window. It was terrifying as he hit and kicked her outside.

I don't know what happened later that night, but usually the police showed up. They could not take my father to jail in those days because it wasn't illegal for my father to be in his own house. The police would have had to witness the fight to make an arrest. They would usually just talk to him and tell him to calm down; but he was always allowed back inside.

We moved back to our house when I was in grade four. I must have been eight or nine years old. The house was not completely finished. The stairs leading to the second floor were only partially built, and you could see through to the basement. Also, the floors were just plywood, and we didn't have any kitchen cupboards. Again, we didn't have hot water, so water had to be heated on the stove and carried upstairs to the bathroom. One night my eldest brother was very badly scalded carrying hot water up for his bath. We all felt so bad for him; he was only a young guy.

The house was much bigger, and we felt good about it. My mother did all the washing in a ringer washer that she moved to the kitchen sink. We took turns helping hang all the laundry on four different clotheslines. Usually it was our clothesline, our neighbor's next door, my uncle's beside the neighbor, and then our other uncle across the street. We had a lot of laundry, and good weather had to be taken advantage of to get the laundry done in one day.

We had a television set that we would rent from a local businessman. He would come collect his payments each week; he was always on schedule. I don't know how often he was actually paid because we had that television repossessed more times than I care to remember. But he would always bring it back when we paid our bill. I remember one day my mother saw him, and she told me to say that she wasn't home. I went up to the wooden storm door when he knocked and said to him through a tiny crack, "My mother said she's not home. Come back later." I could see my mother roll her eyes. I shut the door.

I woke up. I could hear screaming; it was really loud. When I went to bed, my parents and their friends were playing cards at the kitchen table. They were drinking throughout the day and evening. I used to get up in the middle of the night to check that no lit cigarettes were put in the trash or anyplace that could start a fire. On this night, I was awoken by my mother's loud screams. She was really mad and shouting swear words with that voice that is between anger and tears. My stomach instantly became upset; that bad feeling that overwhelmed me when another fight was starting. All had seemed fine when I went to bed, but now my mother had a big knife in her hand trying to get at my father. I don't know who was holding them apart, probably my brothers. But I saw that knife in her hand, and I ran for it. I yanked it out of my mother's hand by the blade. It was probably not that sharp because I didn't do too much damage to my hands. I can still see the light scars on my hands where I yanked it from my mother.

It's weird to think that after all the crazy traumas we witnessed, sometimes during the week, that it was normal to go about our usual business the next day. Whether it was to school or hanging with friends, life just went on. I couldn't imagine how the scenario would have played out if we had a school psychologist or counselor at the time to inquire after our home life. I suppose child protection would have been made aware of our situation. However, for many of us on the reserve, it was just normal. To this day, in any situation that requires quick action or indicates trouble in some manner, my stomach reacts in the same way every time.

All night I talked about hurts, slights, violence, poverty, wants, needs, and rejection, both real and imagined. Every memory every year recalled and examined. I was exhausted. By the time I reached my brother's death when I was fifteen, it was morning.

Chapter 3

As I meditated that morning after hearing the thunderous bang in the house, I was a little nervous on the message that I would receive. I had been receiving guided messages for the past nine months in one form or another. It could be two words or a stream of thoughts that I would need to quickly write down following the meditation. As a vibrational feeling encircled my forehead, I awaited the message. I could feel and sense energy all around me—through my hair, down my back, arms, and legs. These feelings could last anywhere from ten minutes up to an hour, depending on the comfort level of my seating. At times two hours could easily pass before I would release the connection.

A few days before, I was guided in meditation to attend a psychic tea church fundraiser in the local area. The meditation session was particularly strong that evening. I could feel the energies trying to get my attention while I watched television with my family. I said to them, "Sorry, guys, if I don't meditate now, the angels are not going to stop." As I grounded myself, the message was immediate. I was directed specifically by name to one of the mediums who was scheduled to give readings at the psychic tea fundraising event. I had to check the church website to see when the event was scheduled; it was the next morning. However, when I arrived that morning at the church, I was informed that particular medium did readings by appointment only and she was pre-booked for the day. Disappointed, I asked if there was another time when I could see the medium. I spoke to a couple who scheduled her readings and was surprisingly given an appointment at the end of the day. Generally the medium started at 8:00 a.m. and gave readings until 4:00 p.m. Today they would add another appointment at 4:00 p.m., which meant I could see her that day after all, but I would need to come back later. When I returned, the psychic tea had ended a couple of hours earlier, and I was the last one to get a reading.

I previously attended lectures at a spiritualist church, and readings from spirit are common. Over the last couple of years, my spiritual growth was aided by a vast array of books on spiritualism and psychic phenomenon, many of which I had been guided to as I worked through different concepts and issues involved in the healing process. At the time I didn't realize I was going through a healing process. I just thought I was reading because I enjoyed the books. But anytime I had a question, off to the library I would go, and I would return with three or four books that would expand my knowledge on the topic. I would often finish a book in a day, sometimes two. The list of books went on and on. I started organizing my thoughts on poster boards, figuring out what different authors were saying about the afterlife, about our life purpose, about God. What could I say to a person that would make most sense to them? Where could I start the conversation if it presented itself? I knew this was going to happen. Something in me told me to learn how to communicate clearly, with a knowing that would invite the other person to perhaps ask questions but not frighten the person or impinge on his or her sense of reality.

I sat down, and the medium began. The reading was for a half hour. Names were put forward, more as validation that she was connecting with spirits connected to me. All were confirmed. "You know you are very much guided with spirit in many ways," she said. "Do you make people aware of spirit?" she asked. I do, but it is mainly family and only the ones I know are open to messages from spirit. Even then, I'm not sure how the messages are received.

I imagine it's somewhat challenging for my family to engage with me in one manner our entire life and then have our relationship altered by my recent spiritual awakening.

The medium continued, "I see that you get thoughts, you get impressions. I'm going to say why don't you start carrying around a tape recorder or book to record these thoughts because you are going to have the opportunity to put a lot of things together that are going to help people?" She asked, "Who are the men in soldiers' uniforms who were connected to you; I have one that is taller than the other?" I replied that they were my uncles. She said, "They are bringing a beautiful vibration. I feel like I want to say to you that he says nothing is too big, too small, or too awkward for her to handle. She will get through it all! He says if you told her the water was too deep to swim across, she would do it just to prove a point!" We both laughed.

The medium said, "Have you talked about writing a book on your experiences?" I did at one point, but I didn't really want to expose myself. "Well, I think you are going to do a lot of writing and I don't know what's that all about, but I feel good about it. There are a lot of things that you are going to set straight; people are going to finally listen. You are not beating the drums for nothing! Have you been talking about getting a group together to meditate?" she asked. No, I replied. "Well something is going to happen and you are going to draw people to you. There is going to be meditation groups, and you will be surprised what is going to come out of that for you."

She asked, "Did you go home recently and come back with a lot of memories?" I went home for my mother's funeral last September and did come back with a CD of pictures of my mother and father that was played at the funeral reception. "I see a fancy teapot. Who loved their tea?" No, that was a teapot I bought my mother when I traveled to Saudi Arabia in my twenties. I brought it back home with me. I brought home letters my mother had saved that I wrote to her during that time as well. "Well, your mother is just validating that she is here, and she wants everyone to know that everything is all right and that she is at peace. She wants you to know that it was a celebration when she arrived. I feel like I want to say to you that I don't know who did all the dancing, but I feel like I danced all night, if that means anything to you!"

In reference to this last comment by the medium, prior to my mother's passing after a long, often challenging three years in which her health deteriorated, my father, who had passed fifteen years prior, had managed to send a message to my brother through a local medium in our community. A little part of the message indicated that when my mother passed, he would be there to greet her and would dance my mother away.

I had also received a message from a cousin who had passed and wanted to get a message to his mother. He wanted his mother to know that he would be persistent in trying to get her attention until she recognized that life continued after this life. I asked for validation that I could share with her, as I was a little wary of delivering the message to his mom. I didn't know how she would receive it, if she would believe it, or perhaps if she would think I was flaky. The medium said, "Your cousin is saying that he moves things. She thinks she is going crazy, losing her mind, but it is him!" When I passed on the message to his mother, she in turn validated his message by confirming that a statue she had on her dresser drawer in her bedroom was constantly being moved. One moment it was facing one way and the next it was facing another way. After much angst over delivering the message to his mother, it was received in the manner in which it was sent—in much love and laughter that was part of their family bond.

I left the session feeling that perhaps I was guided there by my cousin to deliver the message to his mother. Then a couple days later a new development occurred.

My meditation was deepening. I began to focus; the vibrational circling on my forehead was now pulsating. I was being drawn away, aware of the energies surrounding me. Information was starting to come through. All I heard was, "Write your book."

"About what?" I asked.

"Your life," I heard.

"How long do I have to write it?"

"April 28."

But that was only two weeks away! My mind was reeling. How on earth would I be able to write a book in two weeks?

I started to receive lines that opened with, "I don't know when it all started, but at an early age I was able to ..." It continued. Images flashed in my mind of events, sequences. It was like an outline was starting to take form. I was intrigued. I was getting anxious to start. I walked out of my bedroom and informed my husband that I was going to write a book. He was surprised, not with the concept of writing a book but with the timeframe. He asked, "Do you really think you can do that amount of writing in two weeks? An actual book!"

I was positive that whatever I was guided to do would be a success. I could write a chapter a day. It would get done. I had just come off a very intense project that had a very tight deadline, so I felt confident that it was just a warm-up to what I had to do to write the book. I got out my computer and started to write. That first day I wrote two chapters.

A couple mornings later, I woke up, uncertain of what my dreams were telling me. I didn't feel myself; I felt like I didn't want people to know about my life. The dreams were showing me people who would laugh at me, doubt my story, doubt my validity. I put it aside and started to get ready for the Easter long weekend. It's just my insecurity, I surmised, and went on with my weekend activities. The dreams persisted.

I thought to myself, *I worked through all of these feelings. Why am I now feeling insecure?* I meditated again and asked about the timeframe. Maybe I was wrong. Then I heard, "It's like a Band-Aid. Rip it off quickly!" I knew instinctively what the guidance meant. The book was to be written quickly, so as not to drag out the feelings that I was experiencing in writing the book. My dreams were my own ego, unwilling to let my guard down, to reveal the side of myself that I had kept hidden. I thought about the people who might read this book; what would they think? Was I going to allow my ego to dream up some possible scenario in which I would be humiliated, pointed at, thought of as less of a person because of the life I have led? No way, that already happened, and I wasn't going to let it happen again. Definitely not by me!

I was led back to a little affirmation that I was guided to remember during a meditative healing session. "I am the sum total of all my experiences; to love from one heart … not to be diminished in any manner." In this healing, the two halves of me were recognized, loved, and forgiven. I reached down to bring up and demonstrate love and forgiveness to my other half. She was very small. I cried for her. She was the one who experienced all the lessons. She was the one who was broken, ashamed, embarrassed, burdened, and frightened. I took her hand, and she rose up and joined with me, our blood vessels fusing together to form one heart, beating as one. I loved her.

Chapter 4

The days following my first release session were filled with learning what I could about my husband's traditional culture. These were the traditions in which the healer said we would raise our children. I also spent time reading books that he suggested which would help with understanding the traditional path. I read all these books with fervor. I wanted to do a good job, be a good student. I encouraged my husband to read the books as well. He didn't care to read beyond what was required for business, but he read a couple that I pushed him to read.

The books the healer recommended were mainly on traditional hunting and gathering, tracking, preparation of game meat, traditional code of ethics and morals, and so on. The healer was convinced that an apocalyptic event within the next couple of decades was going to decimate much of the population and that only a few pockets of society would survive; and in anticipation of that event, we had to teach our kids how to survive in the wilderness. The kids needed to be trained to help lead people to caves in areas that were predetermined as locations for the First Nation people to gather. He also directed me to authors of a spiritual nature who supported this theory.

I was excited to read all the books that were suggested by the healer. I thought it would help me accept what was being taught to me. I wanted to learn even more than what the healer had already revealed. I felt it was my duty to understand the traditional ways of my husband's nation. I included additional books into my review, books on traditional ethics and morals that he referenced occasionally. However, I started to notice contradictions from what the healer was teaching to what was stated in the traditional books on ethics and morals and the eternal punishments that would damn all those who did not show observance. He laughed when I brought these up to him, like he had insider knowledge. He was quick to dismiss the literature as uninformed. He said they were written by people without knowledge of the traditional language. The healer was not fluent in his traditional language, so his insistence that these books were uniformed didn't make much sense to me as some parts of the books on morals and ethics he quoted exactly.

At this same time, my dreams were changing; they felt different, more real. They came not every night, but frequently. I got into discussing my dreams with the healer during our sessions together. I would try to interpret the dreams myself using the dream book that I purchased—one that the healer recommended. I would give the healer my interpretation, but he seemed to always have a different meaning. I was confused. I was using the same dream book. Then one night, I had a dream that involved traditional healers. They were seated around a table when I entered the room. One was preparing traditional medicine near the kitchen sink. I sat down, and the healer came up from in back of me and started forcing the medicine down my throat. I was choking. I woke up gasping for air.

When I revealed the dream to the healer, I said that I couldn't find anything in the dream book to help with the interpretation. The healer said anything with traditional medicine could not be interpreted through that manner. He said that in my life, there were going to be four men who would try to use bad medicine on me and that I had to protect myself; they wanted to have me for themselves, and they would attempt in various ways to draw me to them. The healer revealed that certain medicines were used to seduce an individual who otherwise would not show any interest in them. I was not to leave my jacket any place unattended as medicine could be put around the collar; this included my office as well. I also had to watch that no one touched the back of my neck or put anything in my drinks. I could not take anything from anyone such as coffee, tea, water, etc., as it could be tainted with bad medicine.

This freaked me out to say the least. I was heading out of town on business, and he said there would be someone at the workshop who was interested in me and would attempt to seduce me in this manner. Talk about paranoid. I don't think I had my back to anyone the entire trip. I was exhausted keeping an ever-watchful eye for anyone around me. The workshop was packed and I was hosting it, so it was quite a challenge to stay away from anyone who could be seen as suspect. Generally, this was any person of the male gender, and it was a construction trades workshop.

Unfortunately, had I been confident in myself to interpret the dream, I would have understood the message that was being shared with me by my higher self to not trust this healer who was filling me with negative influences. Had I been strong, I could have at this time moved forward on my own spiritual journey, in my own way; however, I did not trust enough in my own abilities to communicate directly with God. As often misinterpreted by the faithful, I felt as though I needed an intervener to help absolve me of my sins. My guilt and fear were continuing to steer the ship, and the healer continued to manipulate this weakness.

I never really showed this guilt and fear to the outside world. It was internal, festering, primed for any illness that could take root. I appeared to those who didn't know me well as confident, outgoing, and perhaps a little conceited. I dressed well to help create an illusion of sophistication. I absolutely did not feel that way as I struggled with my own personal demons. I didn't have my own identity; I was too busy creating one from those around me. I went through life feeling like I was owed something, what, how much, I don't know. Just something!

Driving around town, I started taking note of certain license plates with the same four letters that appeared over and over again. I would stop at the traffic lights, and there they would be! This continued steadily and has not stopped to this day. The license letters were BEVJ. One night I again had a dream that was unforgettable and sent me back to the healer for interpretation.

In the dream I slid into home base as though I was playing baseball, but I was on a toboggan. It stood up, and there were three older native women standing around me. I stood up and asked them if they knew what BEVJ 368 meant! (That was the last license plate I seen that day.) They indicated that they did, and I seemed to be moved forward, but they didn't tell me the meaning. I was then pushed from behind toward a childhood friend. My friend said to me, "Paula, the hawk is coming to help you, and you must be ready!" I moved forward again toward a voice that was speaking to me and I listened intently, but when I woke from the dream, I couldn't recall the message.

The healer interpreted this dream as one in which I was being given direction to participate in a traditional ceremony of his clan that involved the hawk. I thought at the time; this made sense! I felt honored to participate. (Later I would learn from my sister that our own family is from the hawk clan. Since that time, I have had many dreams that involve the hawk; it flies into my window and whispers into my ear.)

When I was finally given the go-ahead from the healer to visit my family, it was five weeks since the healing process began. I was not the same person. I could go home for two days, but that was all. My mother's health was still stable at this time, even though she had a near-fatal bout with flesh-eating disease in which her arm and partial shoulder were amputated. Fortunately, she was able to still live independently and had readjusted to life as an amputee through rehabilitation and support from the community health services unit on our First Nation. It was two weeks before Christmas.

The healer told me that there were many negative spirits around my community because we didn't follow proper burial rites for the deceased. He said some negative spirits were around my mother's home, and they were making her ill by touching her food because she took too long to eat it. He recommended that she cover her food with a white tea towel when she was not eating; this also applied to any food left out on the counter. The earthbound spirits were hungry and would touch her food; they had not lost the appetite for earthly things, such as food, liquor, drugs, or sex. He said some spirits around there were going to want me; they could watch what I was doing and become physical if they so desired. I had to be especially careful when I was asleep as my defenses would be down. I was given protection medicine before my trip.

To say the least, I was scared to be at my mother's home. It no longer felt like my childhood home. The healer had convinced me that the house would require a cleansing, and protection medicine would need to be sprinkled throughout the base of the home. However, he made it clear once again that protection medicine would not work if any person using drugs or alcohol entered the home. My mother would need to request it; I never asked.

Even in our own home, we would not allow people into the house. We would talk to them outside because we didn't know if they did the things that the healer said was forbidden.

That first evening, my mom and I talked into the night. We drank tea and ate sweets that she was so fond of; she had such a sweet tooth. I was very grateful that she allowed me to talk about the traditional path that I had accepted as part of the healing process. She listened to all the traditional concepts that I was sharing with her and simply acknowledged that she was unfamiliar with traditional ways as that was not part of the community in which she or our family were raised. She did not judge. She had been a drug and alcohol counselor for the past thirty years and helped many in our community. I understood at this time that she wanted me to be happy. She knew I was struggling with the past. She knew I needed healing.

Actually, I was afraid to go to bed. The healer said I was to receive from spirit three medicines that I would need to bring home with me; this was a test. I tried to sleep, but I was too unnerved. I could hear my mother slightly snoring down the hall. I wanted to wake her, to tell her what I was really going through, but I thought she would think I was crazy. I wanted to tell her of all my fears—to let her know that I was afraid to sleep alone. It was 2:00 a.m., and I was restless. I needed to sleep to receive the messages, but I couldn't because I was scared of the spirits. It was getting close to morning, and I was panicking. *Oh no, I can't go home without those messages!* I had just the one night in which they would be revealed to me. I texted the healer, who told me to sleep when it got light; he laughed, said I was weak and the spirits kicked my ass.

I slept a couple of hours in the morning but then got out of bed because I had little time to visit everyone. Some family members dropped by to visit throughout the day. It was good to see everyone. I reviewed the traditional path I was journeying and some of the books I had read. As I mentioned earlier, many of these books were focused on apocalyptic and negative spirit activity. I'm happy I was not successful in encouraging my family to read any of them; it is not a positive means by which to begin a spiritual journey.

I know now that fear will only lead you to make temporary or casual changes—changes that will crumble or collapse at the slightest provocation or opposition from family, friends, or even your spouse. All it will take is one suggestion, one invitation, one more time, and you are back to where you first started.

That second night I slept with my mother; I was exhausted. She didn't ask any questions.

I returned home to Ontario and immediately experienced again the guidance dreams. I was in the living room at my mother's home, and I was floating up the stairs. I knew I didn't want to walk down the hall to the bedroom where I had slept. I was standing at the landing at the top of the stairs. I heard a voice behind me say, "Go." I was being pushed from behind but still floating. I reached the doors to the two back bedrooms, but they were closed. I faced forward but pushed open the right door with my hand. I was scared to look inside. There was a young boy standing beside the bed. He was bald, dark skinned, like a monk. I saw my father sitting on the bed; he was holding someone who was ill. He was comforting them; it was compassion. The young boy moved me to the other room. I opened the door. There were babies under the covers—babies who had recently passed but needed to be cared for and loved. This represented a doorway—a doorway to heaven.

Chapter 5

It was 1977, and my mother had quit drinking. I was starting my second release session from where I left off at the first session. It was summer, I continued, and I was visiting relatives in Ontario. I couldn't return home yet because my mother was in a treatment center. I was surprised because I never, ever saw my mother as an alcoholic. I thought alcoholics were people who were drunks. My mother drank, but she still looked after us.

It was her decision to do the twenty-eight-day program. I would have to wait to return home. I had been away for three weeks already and missed my family.

When my mother quit drinking, our life was changed. She became a regular at Alcoholics Anonymous (AA) meetings and later started work as a Native Alcohol and Drug Addictions Counselor. My father still drank, and this created hardships on the family as he would often binge drink. Every few months, my father would go on a three- or four-week bender. He would leave work and just not come home. Each time he would need to enter a detox treatment center because of the effects the alcohol would have on his body. He could not just quit without assistance. He would have DTs (delirium tremens). He would spend anywhere from one week to three weeks in detox depending on the severity of his bender. Sometimes I would see him when I got off the school bus, and I wouldn't even recognize him. He looked like a homeless person. He was usually clean shaven with his hair nicely styled and well dressed; this man was a stranger.

My father's binge drinking would continue for several more years. In this time, we still had a couple of incidences where my father became violent, but they were controlled quickly. We were all older; we could get my father out of the house faster. The police were also more willing to take my father to jail where he would be detained for night. However, my mother was exhausted from the ups and downs and the stress his binge drinking created within the family. Eventually she took matters into her own hands, got a court order, and he was not allowed to return home after yet another binging episode and requisite treatment to regain his health.

My parents' separation lasted six months. It was a relief not to have my father at the house, but we missed him too. We would visit him at his brother's home; he genuinely missed all of us. He wanted to come home, and after some time we would plead with my mother to let him move home. After the separation my father's binge drinking became less intense. He drank, but illness would overtake him sooner. He developed diabetes. He would need to take better care of himself; eventually the drinking stopped.

My brother's illness began with a sore knee. Bradley complained throughout 1978 that his knee hurt. He was a year older than me. My mother would take him to the doctor, but they always advised it was just water in the knee; a needle would be inserted to drain the fluid. My brother played hockey and other sports, so this procedure was not unusual. He lost weight, but that we attributed to his age. He was fifteen and getting much taller. Nothing seemed amiss.

Bradley celebrated his sixteenth birthday in late 1978; he was in grade ten. Early the following year, he got a cold he couldn't shake. His chest was congested, and he was bedridden for a few weeks. He lost a lot of weight at this time. I'm not certain what the doctor attributed the illness to, but it was most likely pneumonia. For a little while, he got better. I remember the night he went to see *Saturday Night Fever*; we all met afterward at a local teen dance club, and he told us about the movie. I was impressed that he got into a restricted movie; he looked so grown up.

I stop writing here. My heart is heavy, and I am struggling with words to capture a personality that was so incredibly vibrant with life that in only writing about his death seems to do him a great injustice. I pray. Dear God, please give me the strength and courage to share our family's darkest moment of grief, loss, and powerlessness in such heartbreak; but also to share the love that was Bradley, his humor, his ingenuity, his drive, his beautiful spirit. Help me, holy Father, write this with integrity, truthfulness, and love. Amen.

Brad worked from an early age. He delivered newspapers but sometimes asked for my mother's assistance when he had difficulty collecting from some customers. Not that she was about to break any knees, just a word or two with the customer. All of his customers were from our small community, so my mother grew up with most everyone on the reserve and felt comfortable seeking them out. He always seemed to have a little cash. He would babysit for friends and help out where he could, but his biggest money maker was his regular after-school job working at a convenience store. It was locally owned, small, and had gaming machines. Not gambling, but a pool table, pinball machines, and a jukebox. We would all hang out there. I used to constantly ask Brad to loan me a dime or quarter to play the pinball machines or a game of pool. He would usually oblige, but I don't know how I ever thought I could pay him back! He worked at the store for three years.

Oh my brother wasn't perfect, that's for sure. He had this way of joking that could strike at your most vulnerable perceived weakness, whether it was a secret, your appearance, or anything you may have felt the least bit insecure about. For me, that was any number of things; he could embarrass me with just a look, but he never humiliated. He knew the fine line between what was considered humor and that which was outright mean. His friends spanned all age groups. He had a special way of connecting with people; they felt immediately they could trust him. He was just a kid in physical years, but his soul was very old. To this day, I am reminded by community members how much Brad meant to them personally, what he did for them, how he helped. He made a difference in our life and in the lives of those in the community.

Bradley's knee started to hurt again. It was April, just before Easter. My mother brought him to the hospital to see our regular doctor, who was working the emergency room. As it so happened, a surgeon was in the emergency department who took a look at Brad's knee and immediately informed my mother that he would like to schedule a biopsy. My mother informed us when she returned home that the surgeon wanted to do a biopsy and she would need to take Brad to Halifax. I didn't understand at the time what this all meant. It isn't like today when a quick search on the computer can tell you everything you need to know in seconds. As a matter of fact, I didn't even really understand cancer. I knew older people often got cancer, but I didn't know anyone our age who had cancer.

My mother traveled to Halifax with my brother for the biopsy. It was a five-hour trip. I'm not sure if they took a bus or the train. It is a blur. My mother stayed with my eldest brother, who lived with his wife in Halifax. Bradley was admitted to the hospital for the biopsy. A few days later, my mother called with the results. It was cancer. Brad would need to have his leg amputated. He had a type of bone cancer called osteosarcoma. My father delivered the news. We were all in shock. We called my sister who lived in Boston to come home. We were barely able to function that day. The surgery was to be scheduled within the week.

A very close friend of the family managed to raise money from community members so we could travel to Halifax to see Brad before surgery. The following weekend, we arrived at the hospital. A few days had passed since we received the news. Nothing had prepared me for seeing Brad so incapacitated. I didn't know his health was starting to decline so drastically. He needed to wear an oxygen mask to help clear out his now-congested lungs. His leg was propped up on a pillow. It was difficult to understand what he was saying. He would occasionally take off the mask to talk, to joke a little, but he was tired. Our family dropped in to see him throughout the weekend. It was difficult to have us all there at the same time; the hospital room was small, and we have a big family. We stayed at a hotel not too far from the hospital. Before we knew it, the weekend was over and it was time to go. We said our goodbyes to Bradley and Mom and returned home. We waited for the surgery to be scheduled.

The surgery was delayed a couple of times. It was now into May. Bradley's lungs were still too congested to undergo anesthesia. My mother stayed by his side the entire time. Finally, we were informed that the surgery was going ahead on May 10. It just happened that it was my birthday; it was a Thursday. My mother called that day to say the surgery went well. Bradley was in recovery, and the surgeon was optimistic that they were able to get all the cancer. It was bittersweet news; I had trouble imagining what my brother's life was going to be like for him with only one leg.

My father was with my mother in Halifax following the surgery. A couple days later, on May 12, my sister was sitting outside on the front step with her friend. His parents were there, standing talking to my sister. She came into the house crying, screaming that Brad had died. It was chaos; I didn't know what to do. We were all caught off guard. I ran into the woods. It was too much to handle. The pain was palpable; we didn't have our usual support system. My parents were with my brother, and our closest aunt and uncle traveled to Halifax that morning with my younger sister to visit my brother. After getting the initial news, I have no memory of what transpired until the day of my brother's wake.

Apparently my brother had suffered a heart attack. A blood clot had formed and traveled to his heart. He died quickly. He was waked at the house, and his funeral was a beautiful memorial to his life.

As usually happens in families that experience a tragic loss, a gap was left in our family, and we each tried to fill that gap in our own way. For me, it was new friends, going to parties, and hanging out. My cousin introduced me to her friends from school who were my brother's age. They knew Brad and they understood the loss; there was no need to fill them in on what had happened. They were there at his wake; I just didn't know them at the time.

The night when we all met, my cousin invited me to a house party. It was the third floor of a house that had been converted to apartments. There were quite a few people from school; almost everyone was drinking. I had a Canadian Club Whiskey. I didn't drink up to that point, so I didn't really know what to select when asked. I sat quietly on a barstool in the hallway. I was chatting with people around me but then noticed my cousin wasn't there; I asked a few people where she went, but nobody knew. This upset me because the house was downtown, and it was my first time at a non-native party.

The whiskey started to hit me. I said to a couple people that I couldn't believe that my cousin left me at a white person's party!

I was about to stand up and see if my cousin was outside, but my foot got stuck on the stool, and I hit the floor. People checked to see that I was okay, and I went to sit on a chair in the kitchen. By now I had two or three drinks and was getting very animated. I was telling a story and knocked an iron off the counter that landed on my head. I started to cry; it was all so dramatic. Apparently my cousin went out to get mix for the whiskey; she hadn't even been gone long. We all remained close for many years.

I started high school the next semester. I was grateful to have friends who were already attending the school. It was easier to fit in with everyone. I started dating, and life seemed to move forward. I hung out with my friends most weekends, so they are the memories that I have of that time period. I asked my mother a few years ago what she went through following Brad's death. She said it was a very difficult period in her life and that she struggled a lot. She said she was happy we had our friends; that we didn't dwell, that we were all able to move forward. I wish today that I could have been there for her; to have shown her more compassion, understanding, empathy. But she had her friends too, and my father, and for that I am grateful.

I worked most summer breaks and got my first job away from my community when I was in grade eleven. I was very excited. A new roller rink was opening in our town, and a lot of people had applied for jobs. I had to go through three interviews, plus a polygraph test, to get the job. I enjoyed working there on the weekends; it was a lot of fun. I even worked a couple of shifts during the week sometimes if they needed extra help. I was able to meet people from all around the area. Normally, I just knew the kids from school. The staff all got along, and we had a great time working together. I was there for three months and fully expected to stay as long as possible. Then one evening I was talking to the manager. He was not from around the area. We were joking around, and I said something like, "Well then why did you hire me?" He said, "Quota!" I didn't know what he was talking about at first. Then he said they were required to hire from minority groups to fulfill a quota. I thought about this for a while but didn't say anything to him. I was upset. Why did I go through the entire hiring process if they were just going to hire me on a quota basis!

I felt angry. I didn't quite enjoy the work anymore. I had never been confronted with that blatant admission before in my life. We had certainly been accustomed to positions that were set-aside for native-only applicants, but we were aware of the program from the outset. It was not long before I left my job at the roller rink. I knew that I would not be given the opportunity to move up to any position in the office, which I had fully anticipated would happen prior to our conversation. I looked around. Other than a couple of minorities, it was mainly Caucasians who staffed the roller rink, and it was mainly Caucasians who did all the hiring. This was something new to me. I never before felt that there could be any barriers to what I set out to do in life.

I then thought about the year before when I started dating. My boyfriend had confided in me that his mother didn't want him coming to the reserve to pick me up for our date. His mother told him that she grew up near the reserve, and she thought it was dangerous; she was afraid he would get hurt. I had spent my entire life playing around the entire reserve. No area left me feeling unsafe; creepy maybe, but never unsafe. I was embarrassed and resented his mother for her ignorance. How dare she judge us! I didn't quite get over that embarrassment. After a time, I began to notice just how poor everyone was, including us. I didn't want to be there; I didn't want to be an Indian.

I graduated high school in the usual three years. However, my last year was scheduled with eight classes, including a night class in grade twelve biology. I had failed to attain the number of credits necessary to graduate in the previous two years. I received special permission from the principal to undertake extra credits. I didn't have any distractions; all my friends had already graduated. The classes were easy when I put my mind to studying. I had applied to university and received admission to the only one I had on my list. It was a small university located in Halifax.

That same year, my mother became ill. Her back was so painful it could be days before she would feel stable enough to come downstairs. She had to be assisted most days and required hot compresses on her back; they were so hot at times that her skin would scald. She didn't care, but we were the ones applying the hot compresses, especially my older sister, who scalded her hands frequently. During this time, my mother was also on medications to help with pain and depression. She was unpredictable most days. I didn't know what to expect when I got home from school. She could be angry, crying, or out cold. This went on for a very long time. I'm positive it lasted at least a year. My older sister bore the brunt of it, but it had an effect on the entire family.

As quickly as the pain afflicted my mother, it was gone. Again, I asked her about this time, and she told me the pain had been related to stress and all the changes that were happening at work. The Native Alcohol and Drug Addictions Program in which she was employed underwent transformational change, and education requirements were applied to all positions. This required my mother to return to school for upgrading at a specialized NADAP Program hosted by a university in Halifax. She did not adjust well to the program, and the stress affected her, mostly in her lower back. Later her job position was changed and she was not required to complete an educational component. She continued in her position for the next ten years.

My parents threw me a big surprise party for my high school graduation. I remember the absolute shock I felt when I walked into the house. I didn't see it coming at all and was actually taken aback and wondered why my friends were in the house. It was a wonderful night that I will remember forever. My high school days were over; I made it through. I started university in the fall of '82.

Chapter 6

While writing the book, I set aside meditating for a few days. However, on this day I was feeling blocked; my writing had no direction. It was all over the place. I sensed the need to meditate, to relax. Reliving past events and finding the right words to share my memories and feelings had been emotionally draining. I closed my eyes.

I felt the energies quickly form around me. I asked for clarification on whose energy I was feeling most strongly near my arm. I was quickly shown an image of a woman slicing apples for an apple pie. The apples were falling into the pie crust that was already laid out. I immediately recognized my mother. I recognized the apples and the way she sliced them, always leaving a little on the core that we would eat. The energy moved around me but mainly focused on my right arm. It moved up and down my arm; I was being gently caressed. I relaxed for a long while as the energy stayed near; I didn't want to break the connection. I could hear my husband preparing for dinner. It was time to let go. This was a new development.

The first time I connected with my mother was a month after she died in September 2013. I felt like I needed some direction. I had just worked through my grief as well as some lingering issues from my childhood. I sensed that it was time to seek out someone who could help validate the intuitive connections I was experiencing. I definitely was not ready to seek out another healer or seer in the traditional sense. Fortunately, I was able to learn a lot on my own, and I focused my own healing; but now I was looking for help to understand where my emerging intuitive gifts were directing me.

I picked up a book at the library that provided resource material on psychics and mediums, and it included a directory of practitioners in Ontario. I was able to locate a few practitioners in our area and decided on one in nearby Hamilton. I sent an e-mail to the medium, but after a couple of days, she still had not returned my call.

As I meditated the following day, I saw an image. It was an image of a woman being knocked off a stool. Then I sensed someone there and asked for a name. "Sylvia," I heard. Sylvia, I questioned? "Yes, she says as in the song; Sylvia's mother says, Sylvia's crying ..." And then she was gone.

I recalled that in the book there was a medium who was profiled who fell off a stool. I thought I would send her an e-mail. I figured she wouldn't get back to me or was probably booked, but I took a chance anyway. I didn't hear from her for a few days. When she did finally call, she apologized for the delay; she had been out west visiting friends. We scheduled a date for a reading.

The medium was a two-hour drive from where I live. My friend Dawn traveled with me. It had been some time since we had ventured out together without the kids. We had a blast. We talked, reminisced, and just enjoyed each other's company. When we arrived at her house, I wanted to be brave, but I admit that I got a little nervous. I thought, *Here I go again sticking my nose where it doesn't belong. Didn't I learn my lesson the last time!* I convinced myself I was there for career direction; I thought this would be easier for my husband to accept as well.

The medium had a warm welcome. I immediately felt at ease as we sat down opposite each other on comfortable wingback chairs. The room was bright and sunny. I had booked an hour-long session. She began, "I immediately see two people who are around you. They would have been very close. I'm not sure if they were parents or loved ones, but they are extremely close to you and I feel that because you are on your spiritual journey, these people are going to be around a lot more than they would normally be because I don't think these people felt that there was a life after this one when they passed. I feel that their belief system was that they were praying that they would go to a good place, but their belief system was when you passed you passed. I feel that they are around you because they are very pleased that you are not just hanging on to the old religion. You are looking for more—searching for more."

She continued, "One of them to me would have been a very religious person in their own way, very religious but at the same time when I say very religious I don't think they were completely tunnel vision. I think that they would have listened to what other people had to say, but not necessarily that that was okay; they would respect where you were coming from, but they still had their own belief system. Now that they are on the other side, they're recognizing that all the religions, there is only one God, and that all religions everybody takes a little piece from here, there, all over ... This person wants to say that they are doing everything they couldn't do while here, and that they are in a good place.

"I also want to say to you that they are very proud of you that you made a lot of changes in the last year, year and a half; you don't dwell so much on the negativity anymore. It's like okay, that happened, but I'll move on from here. I need to keep growing. I can't keep always looking at the dark things; I need to always look at the positive things. I want to say to you that it hasn't always been easy because people haven't always accepted that you're not falling into the same category as they are—that you are always looking for more.

"I want to say to you that you just don't take what people have to say and think, *Oh that's so right*. You have to find out for yourself whether it is right or it is wrong. I would say to you that that is really a great thing that you are doing that because I feel like I want to say to you not only do you not take someone's word for it, but you need to pay attention to your gut feelings about what this person has to say or what this person is teaching because if it doesn't sit right with you, nine times out of ten it's wrong. So whoever's around me is very, very adamant about this. Not only do you observe, you listen, and then you decide if this is for you or not. I feel like this person is saying you will meet many along the way, all right, who are going to appear to be so sincere, appear to know it all, appear to want to have you part of who they are; but what I sense is that you need to be aware of that because you have a special gift, and they're concerned because many will say they can help you, but it is not so much for you as it is for them because they want your energy to help them do these things. You need to be very aware and always put a bubble around yourself so that you keep the energy around yourself so it is not taken by others.

"I am feeling a woman grabbing my hand. She is a grandmother or great-grandmother. She is a worrier, and she is wringing her hands. This woman would have had many spiritual gifts but because of the times and the life, it was always kept very close to her heart, but she knew when people were coming. She knew when things were going to happen; and in her own way try to steer things around to give people warning or try to change things, just a very loving and caring person.

"You will start to write before long. The information you are going to receive you're not really going to want to share with anybody because you're not going to believe what you are writing, all right. But I want to say, just keep the writing because I feel like I could be reading a book and my hand would be writing over here. This is going to come to you down the road. First you are going to be writing what you are hearing, but something tells me that down the road, it could be that either you are going to be reading and you think you are reading a book but your hand will be writing. Or that you can be in deep meditation and when you come back, you found that you had written something. I always want you to have around you a pen and paper.

"Your journey is going to be a very powerful one, all right. Because I feel in another lifetime you were a very gifted person and you had a lot of wisdom and a lot of knowledge, but you were before your time. So therefore, your life was cut short, and in this lifetime you have to complete all the things you didn't complete in the other one. It is only coming to you now because you had to have all those years before in order for you to come into where you are now. I would say to you that the next years are going to be very busy years for you. I feel at times you are going to be sitting there rubbing your head and saying, 'Okay, where do I go from here?' I want to say to you that when the time is right, you will be drawn to either go to this church or that church or this group, and when you do, you will either feel very comfortable or you will think, *Hmm, there's something not right here, but I need to be here,* because you maybe need to be there to see what not to do! Spirit is going to work with you to draw you to where you need to be. They're going to open your eyes to what is good but at the same time may show you what is not good because you need to have both.

"I will say to you, down the road in four to five years, you will be teaching. You will have a group of people who will be coming to you. You will be probably having a home circle or you will be having something.

"Your mother was a feisty lady. She wasn't going until she was good and ready, and even then she was not ready to go; she fought to the very, very end. She was a loving, caring person in her own way but also a very stubborn person … Did your mom do a lot of things with her hands? Was she a baker? The reason I'm saying that is I can smell things, and around Christmas is when she would have excelled. I hear your mom saying that she has few regrets, few regrets; but one of them was she didn't take the opportunities that came her way, but to let you know that when opportunities knock you need to take them, okay! I think your mom was one of these people who always put the family first, always making sure there was enough money for everybody so everybody had what they needed; I believe she would have scrimped and saved and done without herself in order to make sure that the family had things.

"The family home—is the family home where somebody is still living?" I replied that we all have a say on who will live in the house. "Your mother had a sense of humor; she is saying that for everybody to agree is like pulling teeth. She is rubbing her face in her hands; I think that she is happy that she is not there to have to make the final decision.

"Do you have a chief or was there a native chief in your family? At some point was there a native chief in your family! Because you will be drawn to some ceremony here, and when you are drawn to this ceremony here, you are going to meet somebody who's going to have some connection to you. It's like when you meet someone for the first time you know you know them, but you don't know where you know them from because you never met them before, all right. I want to say in another lifetime, you two were very connected, okay, whether you were sisters, brother or sister, or I don't even know if it is male or female; I just know that you are meeting this person, and you are going to know. But I feel it has to do with some reserve here. I just feel that you're going to have a strange handshake, and your mother is saying it will be good.

"I just feel that in the coming months, you will be more peaceful than you have been in a very long time, and that is because your mom is around you and she is trying to steer you in the right direction." The session came to a close.

As I was getting ready to leave, I casually mentioned to the medium the meditation regarding *Sylvia* and how I came to select her to book a session. She was surprised; her friend's mother had recently died, and her name was Sylvia. Her friend was looking for a sign about whether to take her mother's remains to England for burial with her father.

I drove home that day with mixed feelings. I was familiar with all the concepts discussed in the session, and I also knew the commitment to spiritual practice that was needed to fulfill that journey. Everything started to make sense; the direction I was seeking was provided. All the way home, two hawks remained in our sight. I was certain it was my parents.

Chapter 7

"I have to see you immediately," the healer had texted. "It's very important!" I was at work but agreed to drop by at the end of the day. I was on pins and needles the whole day. I made sure to have forty dollars for the reading and went to his house. It was nearing the Christmas holiday. He said he had a dream, a vision, and it wasn't good. It concerned our boys. He said he saw a white work van with dark windows and somebody grabbing and kidnapping my boys. They would not be able to survive the kidnapping. This would happen in our neighborhood, and it was imperative that we move! We had to move to a community where my mother-in-law had land; there the boys would be safe. I was paralyzed. He said some other stuff after that, but I can't recall what. I had to get home. Oh my God, this was too much handle. How was I going to convince Mark to sell the house!

My husband understood my terror, and he too felt like things were out of control. We questioned everything and went through different scenarios all night. Could this be true! But by the end of the night, we didn't want to take any chances. We decided to put the house on the market immediately. There were no ifs, ands, or buts about it. We were not going to risk putting our boys in harm's way if there was any way we could avoid it.

It just so happened that I had been in touch with a Realtor regarding a house I had been interested in viewing in a nearby neighborhood. I made an appointment with him, and he came over the next day. The house was all ready for sale and didn't require any work. So he took some pictures and drew up a contract, and in a few days our house was on the market. The viewings started immediately. I didn't let the kids out of my sight. If they played outside, we were always with them. I couldn't wait to move out of the house.

It took us six weeks to find a buyer. We signed the deal, and our move-out date was set for April. But where would we live?! The healer was adamant that it had to be in the community where my mother-in-law lived. Rentals units are very sparse in that area; we had to think of something else.

In the time our house was on the market, the healer was providing us direction on where we could build. My mother-in-law had twenty-six acres of land, but there was a problem with the parcel of land we had selected. The healer said we could run into problems if we built there because there was a curse on the land. We had other restrictions too; we could only use the cash from the house sale to build the new house. In addition, the house would need to be very modest and built only big enough to meet our basic needs. We would have to build most of the house ourselves. It could not go any deeper than four feet into the ground. It had to be built before Christmas of that same year. We could not get a mortgage.

We were floored. How could we do this and pay for all the release sessions, the ceremonies, the readings! It seemed an impossible task to complete. On top of all this, the healer also told me to return to school in the fall. I felt like we were both going to lose it—like our marriage was going to crack under all the stress. Could this really be happening?

(I already planned to return to school; I even had the program selected. This information was generally known by people who were close to me.)

Of course, in the weeks leading up to our closing date for the sale of our home, the curse on the land was resolved by a very expensive ceremony. We could build on the land after all. But still, the question of where we would live while we built our house remained an outstanding concern. My mother-in-law's house is built in a loft style and has only one bedroom, so her home was out of the question. We could rent a trailer, but it would cost $1,500 a month, plus we would need to pay fees to set up a septic and cistern for the trailer. We could not afford all these extra costs and build the house at the same time. Our budget was very limited.

I thought I could get around the money shortfall by taking on extra contracts, but the healer told me this could not be done as it would take time away from the boys during weeknights and weekends. Plus additional work by my husband was out of the question; he had to build the house plus do his regular job.

I was in a meeting one day and happened to mention to a lady sitting next to me about our need to rent a house. By this time it was March and getting very close to our deadline to move out of our home. She mentioned that her brother had a house that was empty, and he sometimes rented it out to family. She could ask him if he would consider renting it to us. I was so excited to hear this; at this point, I was willing to rent any home that wasn't rat infested.

She gave me the address and said to have a look before she called her brother. The house was beautiful. It was thirty-five hundred square feet and sat back in hickory trees on about fifty acres of land. There was a veranda that surrounded the home; it looked stately. I hurried back to the office and told her we were interested in renting the house. Could she contact her brother right away! I hoped the rent wouldn't be too high.

We heard back in a couple of days. Her brother was happy to rent it to us, and we could have a look that day. I was happy for the first time in a long while. We arranged a time to look at the house, and we all went to the viewing together. It was larger than I had even first imagined. The kids loved it on sight. It had hardwood flooring and was huge inside. A chandelier hung down from the front entry with a window to showcase the light; it looked majestic. The upstairs section hadn't yet been floored, but temporary carpeting could be put in place. The bedrooms were all painted, and blinds were on all the windows. It had five bedrooms in total. The kitchen and living room comprised most of the main floor, with a den in the back area. I was in love.

My husband handled the rent. He spoke with the owner directly, who offered it at $700 per month. That was exactly our budget. I was ecstatic!

We all thought we would feel miserable to move away from the home we had lived in for nine years, but we didn't—not exactly. We would miss the conveniences of living in the city, but we had to move on. We had to do this; there was work to be done. Prior to moving into the house, my husband needed to go through the cleansing and protection activities that we were directed to do at our old house. Some of it had to be done at night, right at dusk, so he was kind of nervous going around the perimeter of the new home and not being seen by neighbors.

We moved into the rental house the third week in April. The kids slid across the hardwood floors as we placed the first of our items in the vast kitchen of the new home. I had always wanted a big home, and I would get to live in one—at least for a little while.

I felt like a child. It was exciting. We all felt the excitement. My husband was anxious to move in as well. We couldn't look back. I handled retrieving the final items from our house in the city. I said my good-byes and looked at the boys' bedrooms one last time. A brief sadness overwhelmed me; this is where they grew up, and this is where we shared so many memories of when they were babies. I quietly walked downstairs and retrieved our hamsters. They were the last to go; I packed their cages in the car and took one last glance at the house. Good-bye, my home; be good to the next owners.

When we were settled into the rental house, we started our search for a builder. A lady at work mentioned that her niece's husband was a builder. He built her house, and she was very satisfied with his work. We arranged to meet with him the following weekend. We explained our situation to him and let him know that we had a limited budget and he could only take the build to a certain point before we had to take over. I shared some designs that I found online for smaller homes. The house would be no bigger than a thousand square feet. However, the build I selected had vaulted ceilings and a walk-out basement, so it was still like a two-story build. We agreed to work together and prepared our contract.

His only stipulation was that the outside of the home would need to be complete. It could not be left in an unfinished state due to his building standards for his business. His signage advertising his business was on the property. He agreed he would take the home to a finished state on the exterior but only build to a framed state on the interior, with electrical and plumbing roughed in and the shower installed. My husband and I would do the rest. He brought us the architectural design of the house based on the initial design I had provided. They reshaped the design to add some extra square footage and maximize the space. It was beautiful. It would be built into the hill next to my mother-in-law's home overlooking the river.

Prior to the contractor being hired, the healer was constantly bringing up doing the job as a contractor himself. He worked construction for many years and could easily do the job. His wife even suggested that we should consider him as our building contractor. I brought this up with my husband but asked the healer to speak directly with my husband about anything related to the construction bids. The healer always seemed to filter everything through me; he would never ask my husband directly.

My husband said no. There was no way he would entertain having him as a building contractor. What if we didn't like his work? What if he didn't do the work in the time we needed! It was an outright conflict. How could he even suggest such an arrangement? It was unethical. What if we had to fire him? No, definitely not. I was not disappointed. I delivered the message; we were going with the building contractor we had already selected.

Later the healer brought up the bid during a session with my husband; again he reiterated his concerns. The healer said he was a professional; he could separate the healing work from the construction project. It would not create any problems. Again, Mark said no.

Chapter 8

As the release sessions continued, they were interspersed with different types of ceremonies. The traditional ceremonies were primarily to assist us in our life journey and the obstacles we would encounter and offer us protection. I had two ceremonies, and my husband had three. Each of these ceremonies cost anywhere from $500 to $1,100, depending on the type. They were usually paid a week in advance.

I didn't mind the ceremonies; they seemed legitimate enough and involved other people who were truly dedicated to carrying out the ceremonies that were requested and needed by community members. However, I struggle with the fact that I received these ceremonies and wonder if perhaps they were even meant for me. I don't distrust the people who helped with the ceremonies because I believe their intent was genuine; but I question the integrity of the healer and wonder if he was engaging us in the ceremonies as a way to manipulate us further. I will never know, but I respect the gifts nonetheless.

The ceremonies in a way created a tiny crack in the healer's assertions that all information was coming from my spirit guide. One evening prior to a release session, the healer did his usual reading and indicated to me that now that I had three ceremonies, I could move forward to learn medicine, but I had only two. Shouldn't he have known this information!

We started that night's release session where we ended at the last session; I was about to start university. I attended a small university in Halifax. I was unprepared for the transition. My parents didn't travel with me to Halifax. I carted my luggage and trunk into a taxi when I arrived in Halifax and made my way to the university. I didn't really know what to do with my things when I arrived; the taxi driver just left them near the door. After searching around the residences, I finally located security and asked if there was space available to keep my luggage until I finished the registration process. It was midafternoon, and I was tired.

I walked toward the residence registration, approached a girl I thought was friendly, and asked her if she could direct me to the line to register for the apartment style dorms. She indicated that this was the line and that she had just arrived as well. We chatted while we waited. The apartment dorms were a high-rise unit with over twenty floors. The line took a long time, but we didn't mind; we chatted the whole time. When we reached the front of the line, we split into different directions. When we met up again later, it turned out that she was my roommate. She was a few years older and enrolled in an advanced program, but we got along great.

I made a few friends in the first couple of months and did well enough in my courses, and everything was going well. But then things changed. A relationship in which I was involved the previous year ended when he graduated college and moved away, but then I received a call; he had relocated to Halifax. We picked up where we left off. It seemed to be going well until it wasn't. Abruptly he ended the relationship, which seemed to turn my life upside down. I didn't want to stay; it was difficult to be there. The worst thing was that when I ran into his friend at home during the holidays, he informed me that my ex-boyfriend had eloped over the Christmas holidays. I didn't return to school.

I didn't tell anyone what had happened. I just moved home. My parents didn't really mind because they didn't want me to move away in the first place. I returned to university the following two and a half years, but I didn't make enough credits to graduate in the three-year program in which I was enrolled. I had some problems during this time and could not seem to focus my life. It seemed I just moved from one problem to another.

I fit in, but I didn't. Not in my head. I felt too insecure to connect with anyone I could consider a friend to confide in and seek support. Don't get me wrong—I knew a lot of people and would often hang out in groups, but I didn't have friends. I dated one person most of my years in university, but that too was doomed to failure. Deep down, I always felt he was better than me. His family was close knit, with none of the family violence or financial stressors that I had experienced throughout my life. They were educated and socially confident. I came to resent what he represented—a social class system that I didn't belong to and couldn't quite get!

After a couple of years, I began to manipulate every relationship and every situation to ensure I got from it what I needed. I took what I wanted and didn't care who got hurt. It was a dog-eat-dog world, and I was hungry.

As my mind-set changed and I fully embraced this new and more aggressive personality, I moved to Toronto. It was easy not to feel. I wandered in and out of people's lives like a plague. I was in it for myself, and if you happened to come across my path, you would most likely remember me.

I was fun to be with and would not appear in any way to be a menace, but I did have a dark side. I didn't care about you, only what you could do for me in that moment. In my mind, I was going to hurt you before you ever had a chance to hurt me. I couldn't even begin to remember the lies I told or who I told them to; I just let people talk until I knew what they were about. Everybody seemed to want to talk about themselves and impress; I usually knew fairly quickly what they desired and who they wanted me to be! By this time I was twenty-four, and life was one big party. I didn't have friends, but I had a lot of acquaintances I would hang out with at clubs.

My family saw the change in me, but I didn't care. I felt I was living the life and they were just jealous. I was living the life all right but not how I told it! I had nothing. I moved from place to place, never really settling. I was often destitute. I had little by way of material things and always rented furnished rooms until I couldn't pay the rent and would need to move again. I worked, but I also partied. It was more important for me to go out clubbing than it was to pay the rent. I just thought I was owed something in life; I swear if someone offered me their soul, I would have taken it!

Then I hit what I thought was the big time; I was going to Saudi Arabia to work as a flight attendant in Jeddah. It was exactly what I wanted to do. I had always wanted to be a flight attendant, and when this opportunity presented itself, I was not going to turn it down. My parents were very concerned; they thought I was going into some type of white slavery situation that I didn't know enough to avoid. For me, I just wanted to get as far away as possible. I wanted to see the world. After all, I deserved it!

I arrived in Jeddah, and everything was as I imagined. On the way from the airport, I admired the huge homes that peaked out from behind the secured compounds. The walls were eight feet high. We were housed at a female-only section of an

American compound. I shared an apartment with four girls. The accommodations were very nice, and the grounds were well maintained. There was a swimming pool and recreation area located in our section; I think the female compound had three to four sections. Many of the girls were quick to find out where the parties were located from other girls who had already completed a contract with the airline in previous years.

Even though the country is considered dry, there are many places in which liquor is available. However, if you are caught, it could lead to your deportation. Many of the girls had hooked up with groups of people, often from the male American compound. Others got to know some of the locals and would head to their homes where parties were held. I fell in this latter group. It was safer and a lot more discreet. I didn't think I would have any booze during my stay in Saudi Arabia. I truly thought it was dry and was quite prepared not to drink for the length of my contract.

I did have a lot of fun and seriously wanted to get to know the country. I enjoyed the visits to the lavish homes with all their high-tech gadgets, vehicles, and servants. It was like nothing I had ever seen. I wanted to see more of the country; I wanted to go out to restaurants and really experience the country. Unfortunately, I was limited, but I managed to integrate to some extent. I learned the local ways and could easily move around assisted by a hijab and a few of my friends. I went to restaurants along the beach, each a little gazebo separated by curtains. It was beautiful. I went swimming in the Red Sea and drove around the countryside. I wanted to stay.

I traveled to countries near Saudi Arabia situated along east Africa, United Arab Emirates, and India. I often stayed overnight in Cairo and was lucky to be booked on these trips regularly. The hotel where we stayed had a night club, and it was a big party every time. I would always think to myself that it couldn't be real. I couldn't be in Egypt; it was like a dream. I received good reports on my employment records, and it wasn't long before I was seriously considering staying longer in Saudi Arabia. It was a good fit.

My first layover in Cairo was memorable. We had been in Saudi Arabia just two or three weeks and had just finished the remainder of our training. The first part of the training took place in Toronto. A lot of the girls were heading out to party that night, but I had been booked on my first layover in Cairo. I was scheduled to be away for three days. The evening I left for airport; word reached us that there was a big arrest, and over twenty Canadian girls were arrested. They were in jail.

I didn't give it much thought; I believed they would be out in no time at all. However, they were jailed for several days. Word broke in Canada, and my family thought for sure I was among those arrested. They couldn't reach me or get clarification from anyone at the compound on my whereabouts. There worry escalated, and they made contact with the Canadian embassy, but there was still no news on my whereabouts.

It was a long few days for the girls who were arrested. They were released before I returned, but they were all immediately deported.

There was a message to call my mother. I thought something happened at home and had no idea the news of the arrest made it to Canada. I finally connected with my mother and explained the situation to her. I was sorry to have worried her. I didn't have a clue the story was so big. But I was still not deterred. I was excited to be there, and I wanted to take advantage of every opportunity to continue my contract beyond the completion date.

I was there for three months before I slipped up. I was getting comfortable in making the transition from the bus that dropped us at various locations for shopping and into a waiting car with my friends. It was all so easy. The car had curtains, so I only had to make it to the car. Then this one day they were late. I waited near the mall doors. The religious police and others approached me to ask if I needed a taxi; I said I no. I didn't even realize they were watching.

After waiting about forty-five minutes, I saw my friend get out of the car and walk toward me and turn abruptly. I too stopped and walked back toward the mall. It was too late. I was quickly apprehended and taken into a location in the mall. The police were searching my bag. They took my passport. They were very upset. I was then taken to a police vehicle that was parked outside and put inside. I was in there for over twenty minutes in the extreme heat.

I continued to say I didn't know the person who walked toward me and that it was all a mistake. I was taken to a police station. I remember being led to an older area that was sort of like an interrogation room. As I sat in the room, I kept getting hit in the head with a long bamboo pole. It was more annoying than painful. They continued their questioning; I still denied that I was waiting for anyone. Finally I was taken to another building; it had offices.

I was seated in front of a lieutenant colonel. He wanted to know what happened. I was pissed off by this time; I was tired of all the contradictions. Yes, I was going out on the boat, and yes, I was being picked up by my friends. "I'm tired of this," I said. "I see other girls getting off that bus and getting into cars every time I go out. What was the difference today?"

"You should have got right back on the bus when your ride wasn't there to meet you immediately," he replied. "You made it obvious that you were waiting for someone. They couldn't avoid it; too many other people noticed you waiting."

I was screwed. The airline was finally called to notify them of my detention. I think it was three or four hours since I was taken into custody at the mall.

The officer asked why I didn't cry throughout the ordeal. He informed me that most girls would cry and get extremely agitated during their detention. "It's not so bad," I said. "I've been through worse and been in far less desirable accommodations than what you had available."

We had some time. It would be a few hours yet until the airline officials could arrange my release. I started to relax a little more; he seemed like a nice guy. He asked me about Canada; where was I was from? I said, "I grew up on a reserve. I'm not sure if you are familiar with the Indian reservations in the United States; our reserve system is somewhat similar." He did, and he wanted to hear more.

"Are you hungry?" he asked. He called in an elder to sit with us. We would have some tea.

He went to school in the United States. One of his favorite things to do on his time off was travel to various Indian reservations around the country. He thought the culture was fascinating. We chatted for a few hours, and he told me about the places he had visited; it was after 10:00 p.m. when everything was finalized for my release.

It was around 11:00 p.m. by the time I arrived back to the compound. The Canadian team that recruited and organized flight attendants for Saudi Air were waiting. They asked, "Are you okay! Did they hurt you?" They couldn't believe that it was me who was taken into custody.

To them I was quiet, worked hard, and did as I was directed. They suspected I went out, but I kept it low key and made all my curfews. I didn't give them any cause for concern. My flights were cancelled. I fully expected to be sent home the next day, but I wasn't. I was informed that I would be grounded for the next few days and they would keep me updated.

The next day I got a phone call from my friends. They wanted to know if I was okay and said they were working with the authorities to get everything sorted. Later that week I was called to the airline's administration office at the airport. My passport was returned to me, and I was put back on the flight schedule. I was scheduled to work a flight the next day.

"You were very lucky," the manager said. "I don't know what happened, but everything has been cleared up, and there will no further actions in regard to this matter. I will expect that you will be more discreet in the future," he said.

"Definitely," I replied.

I stayed to finish up my contract, but I was no longer interested in a full-time position. I was looking forward to returning home. The rose-colored glasses had been removed. The reality of the situation and the manner in which religious infractions were dealt with was something I didn't want to mess around with. I was in their country and had to follow their laws; I realized that I had no control. I went out a few more times, but I was content to leave any partying to when I was out of the country on layovers. This was far safer, and I didn't need to constantly look over my shoulder.

I returned to Toronto and picked up where my life had left off. I immediately found a job, and for the next year or so everything was on track. I still went out two or three times a week, but it was different. I didn't feel like I needed anything from anyone; I was just enjoying being me. For this brief time, it seemed I was going to make a go of it. I was becoming confident in my ability to look after myself. Then I had an injury that took me out of work; it was long enough to send me spiraling again. My life shifted back to the old ways. Back to the dog-eat-dog world of my earlier years. There were gaps in time, sometimes months, in which I wouldn't contact my family. They worried that I had fallen victim to some murderous individual. I didn't care; I was too lost to care.

Finally, as I approached my twenty-seventh birthday, I realized my life was truly falling apart and going nowhere. I needed stability.

I decided to move back home with my family; it had been ten years since I left.

The first year was definitely an adjustment to all concerned. I was still in that fight-or-flight frame of mind and returned to Toronto a couple more times. The third time I returned home to Cape Breton, I stayed. I realized I really wanted to be home. I was getting to know everyone again, and my family helped with the transition. I still didn't have any thought as to what I was going to do with my life, but I was finally stable. I could finally relax, and I felt a little more at ease. I started to do contract work for my aunt. It was office support, but I enjoyed it.

The transition away from my old life was gradual. I reconnected with my siblings and all my childhood friends. I was finally losing the sense that I needed to impress all the time; I was good enough. For two years I was supported, cared for, and loved by my family, relatives, and friends. It was all unconditional; no one was looking for anything in return. The community I despised when I left was now my refuge.

Chapter 9

Two days before the deadline to finish the book, I was getting ready for bed and brushing my teeth. I could feel a sensation on my left calf. I swiped at it a couple of times, but nothing seemed to be there; it continued until I finished. I was very tired and knew I would fall asleep quickly; I felt myself relaxing, almost like I was floating. Then I felt a thud on my pillow right next to my face. I opened my eyes; I stared, hoping that whatever was there would manifest. I could feel the heaviness on my pillow next to me. After a half hour, I finally decided whomever was there was not going to manifest. I went to sleep.

The next day I attended services at the spiritualist church. It was a beautiful, uplifting service. Near the end, a woman who often officiated at the church shared a message with me from spirit. I am paraphrasing here as I didn't take notes. She said, "I see a big dog sitting next to you. It appears to rest his head near you." She demonstrated this with her hands resting under her chin. "It's like a dog who has put his head on your lap. He represents unconditional love. The angels are going to share with you much unconditional love. It is a gift. You, in return, will share and demonstrate unconditional love in your life. Open your heart."

This past February, after I had been attending the spiritualist church for several weeks, I felt particularly tearful while attending a Sunday church service. I felt as though I would burst into sobs at any moment. I knew my life was better than it had been for a long while, and I was very busy working on a project I loved. But obviously something was up. Usually I felt light—unburdened. People would often comment that I had a wonderful energy around me, so why the tears!

Following the church service, I sat with the same woman during the fellowship tea. I casually asked if she did any counseling. Well, it wasn't really casual; I was still feeling quite tearful, and it was obvious. I asked if she could meet with me sometime soon; she was a spiritual counselor. She happily obliged, and we arranged to meet in the next couple of weeks. We met in the church. Beautiful meditation music played in the background. She asked me what was on my mind. It all came pouring out, the guilt, resentment, and recriminations for not being smart enough to see how I had been manipulated, duped, exploited by a healer. "I worked through all of this!" I exclaimed after my outburst. "Why am I still feeling such negativity about that time in my life?" I truly felt I had forgiven—that I had let go of what happened and was moving forward with important lessons learned from the experience.

"There is something else that you are not seeing," she said.

We talked about forgiveness, love, and what we unknowingly attract into our lives because we think we deserve it for whatever reasons we conjure up to keep ourselves from growing to maintain the status quo. At this time, she recommended a book titled *You Can Heal Your Life* by Louise Hay, but I didn't remember. I was too caught up in that moment's angst to write it down.

We arranged to meet again the next week. She asked how my week went. I explained to her the revelation I had on the drive over to see her.

I didn't forgive myself! I went through a process of forgiving everyone else, but I didn't forgive myself. I didn't even consider that I needed to forgive myself. I couldn't truly love others because I didn't love myself. I was just going through the motions. I understood all the spiritual concepts, but I wasn't applying them, most especially to myself. My world opened up that day.

"Forgive yourself," she said. "You made the decisions you did with the knowledge you had at the time. We would all love to have twenty/twenty hindsight, but that is not available to us. We are on this earth plane to learn our lessons, to experience life, both good and bad. It is what we take away from those experiences that help us grow to help us fulfill our life purpose in this lifetime.

"By the way," she asked, "did you read the book I recommended?"

"No," I replied. I wrote down the information and purchased it a few days later. I read it in one sitting. Then I went back through the book to complete some of the self-healing exercises that were recommended and started on that too. But something stirred; I had done a lot of this work already!

During the church service the following evening, a message from spirit was given to me. *I was not to look back. Look ahead; good things are going to happen.* I knew this part of my healing journey was complete. The exercises were not necessary. However, as clarified in the book *You Can Heal Your Life*, we never stop the healing process. Healing is part of our life journey.

I believe as we awaken to our spiritual knowledge, it becomes essential to incorporate daily healing into our lives to ensure we're not creating imbalances in our minds, bodies, and spiritual connectedness. Energies cannot access an overloaded vessel or busy mind. Even then we may need to call upon others for assistance when the challenges are too great and we are at risk of overwhelming ourselves, for it is in these moments of weakness when we are at greatest risk of stepping off our paths.

That night I danced around the kitchen, I sang, and I laughed; my life was changing. I goofed around with my family, and my happiness was contagious. I was referred to as Happy Feet! I loved it, and I loved my family. The joy I was experiencing was real. I saw beauty in everything and gave my thanks to the universal energies that whispered their guidance to me, that whispered in the ears of those who helped me, that whispered into the ears of those who supported me, and for all the guidance yet to come.

A couple of weeks after my sessions ended with the spiritual counselor, I was meditating, and I kept hearing the name Louise Hay. I recognized it as the author of the book I had just finished. I thought, *E-mail her!* I thought this was crazy. Why would I have any reason to e-mail Louise Hay? It persisted all morning and through the day. Finally I said to myself, "Okay, just look up her name and see what comes up." I typed in her name, and the first thing that popped up was a Hay House conference, I Can Do It 2014: A Conference to Help Energize Your Mind, Body, and Spirit. It was scheduled for the following weekend in Toronto. I booked it immediately. I was so excited; the authors on the speakers' list were ones with which I was familiar. I was also surprised to learn that most of the books I read were published by Hay House. I didn't even notice that fact until that point.

I set out the next weekend to attend the conference. I brought some of my books along just in case there was an opportunity to have them signed by the author. I went alone but soon connected with three other women seated near me. We were all meeting for the first time. We had a great time chatting about what brought us to the conference, our work, and what we were hoping to get out of the workshops. For me, I knew guidance had led me to this conference, so I was curious to see why!

It was brilliant. The speakers were vibrant, and their energy radiated the stage. I laughed, cried, and rejoiced at the amazing fortitude and resilience of the speakers and at their continued awe and gratitude for the beautiful gifts of spirit that provided them with guidance. The venue was packed, but it was like each speaker spoke directly to me alone. Their messages resonated with love. I leaned over to one of the ladies I was sitting with and said out of the blue, "One day I'm going to be on that stage too!" She looked back at me and without even blinking an eye replied, "I believe you!"

At one of the book signings, I received a beautiful angel message to, *"Follow my guidance."*

I returned home inspired and reenergized. I had a busy week ahead of me. A big project report was due on the Friday, and I was still trying to get as many people as possible to complete the survey that was part of the project. It was a targeted survey, so only certain health professionals could participate. I would attend one more conference, but it was close to my deadline. I was really pushing it; if I didn't get any surveys, it would have been a big waste of time. I knew for a while the exact number of surveys I would collect. It was revealed to me during meditation.

It was the second day of the conference, and we still hadn't got the surveys I needed. The conference would last only another few hours, and my survey would be closed that evening. My best friend was there with me as she assisted me in promoting the surveys. I needed six more. My friend is very open and also believes in the power of prayer. I took her hand and said a short prayer to our angels. I said to her to repeat after me, "One and one and one!" She did. Two minutes later the first of the six targeted participants approached the table to complete the survey. I thanked the angels again for their assistance. We talked about it all the way home.

Chapter 10

The build on our new house was right on schedule. It went up quickly. The contractor was finished with his part of the build in just six weeks. From the outside, it looked complete. The daunting task of finishing the interior was now on my husband, as well as making the budget work for the remainder of the build. There would also be additional costs to install the cistern and the septic units, which were estimated at $11,000. At the same time, the healer was pushing for him to do additional release work. My husband had already finished. He said there was honestly no more to talk about! The healer pressured me. "There are things he needs to talk about. He's going to cheat on you," he said. I couldn't tell my husband any of this but only ask him again to consider the release sessions. This was in July.

The pressure was mounting. Our budget was tight, and I was still being asked to do release work. It seemed there was always more that I had to review; the healer would tell me my guides were saying I was not telling him everything. I finally reached a point where I didn't have any more to tell. I racked my brain trying to remember things he said I had overlooked. The extra costs were creating more stress on our marriage. My husband postponed additional release work, and boy did I hear it from the healer. "Your husband is hiding things!" However, the healer still did nothing to communicate directly with my husband. It was all on me.

At this point, I had been married to my husband for seventeen years. I knew a lot about him, and he is pretty much an open book. The things the healer was saying about him and what I knew about him didn't make sense. Then the healer told me my husband's guides were getting angry and that they would soon teach him a lesson due to the delays. I wanted to scream; I was tired of this crap! The ironic thing is that the healer would delay many of our sessions because his schedule was busy or something last minute would need to be handled. Our guides didn't seem to be angry when he postponed!

July moved into August, and I was trying to work through my feelings about the healer. He shared a lot with me about other clients he had and would often tell me who they were and what some of their issues were. This put me on edge because if he was talking about them then he could be sharing information about us! He seemed to enjoy the secrets. He would tell me things my husband said in release sessions and what another person close to us said. It didn't seem right.

In a dream, I was walking with a young man. He had knocked on my door. I didn't know whether to speak to him, so I joined him outside. My house was covered in an embroidered purple fabric. It was beautiful. We walked for a while, chatting as we moved along; he was pushing a bike. He gave me his name, but I didn't recognize it. He was wearing a cream or white cable knit sweater, but it was all wet. The sleeves were all stretched. He had red hair, and I remember thinking that he was very tall for his weight because he was quite skinny. *Could anyone be that skinny?* I thought. We walked toward the river, and then we parted ways. As I returned home, there was a text on my BlackBerry from my husband to not open the door to the stranger. I walked in the house and woke from the dream.

I wrote down his name and some of the details of the dream immediately. It was a Thursday in August 2011. The next week I was reading the paper online when I came across an article about a missing person. It was the same guy who appeared in my dream. I ran to check the date of my dream and the name I had written. It was the same. I became ill. It was all too much; I got sick and started to vomit. After I calmed down, I reviewed the details of the dream with my husband. I had already discussed the dream with him on the morning it happened; the name was a little unusual, and I asked if he knew anyone by that name.

I didn't know what to do. I went for a drive and looked along the river banks close to the area I thought had appeared in my dream. Then, feeling upset, I went to the healer to try to get some clarification on the dream. He immediately said the person was dead and that he would be found in the river. I shouldn't look for him. He would be discovered in a short while. Further, he said he was being shown that I would help people find loved ones in the future. He had to help me with this gift, and I needed to use medicine to help with my development. He was very proud of himself and said he had never before helped anyone get so far in developing their psychic abilities.

The boy was found the next day—alive and well. I was relieved, but it opened my eyes. The healer was wrong. I saw this as a sign. I had been seeing the healer for nine months; my trust in him had weakened significantly, and this was another nail in the coffin. I had later learned that the boy had suffered a head concussion and became disoriented and ended up in another city six hours away.

Fortunately, at this same time I was led to a different kind of spiritual guidance in books I found at the library. They were focused on love, forgiveness, spiritual healing, angels, mediums, near-death experiences, and the other side. They were beautifully written and inspiring—nothing like the books I was asked to read by the healer. These new books opened a door; I was captivated. I read all night and sometimes would read passages to my husband. These books made sense; I read as many as I could that August.

I went to the healer only a couple more times after I read about the missing boy. My husband and I were both approaching the end of our yearlong healing process, and the healer told me we needed to focus on meditation and preparation for the final release session. The final healing sessions would be performed individually, and both were expensive. The sessions would include an overnight stay in the woods to eliminate any fear we had and would mark the end of the healing process. A final element of the ceremony would include silver coins that we needed to purchase.

I was scheduled for the meditation sessions which again were very expensive; my husband was too busy to attend any more of the sessions. I tried to meditate and open my third eye, but it was not working. I was finally asked to sit on a bench under a tree. I sat there for an hour, and a bunch of nuts hit my head. The healer said he was getting me used to the woods for the overnight sessions. He cleaned his yard.

A second session was scheduled, but that too didn't work. I could not relax. His talking irritated me. This was the last time I would see the healer.

Chapter 11

The release work turned in a different direction; I was finding it difficult to completely focus on the negative. I was reaching a point in my life where I had started creating more balance; it was a period of positive change. I still had negative emotions to talk about, but they were not all hate filled like in my earlier sessions. I began my review of this period.

I enjoyed being back in Cape Breton; the year was 1993. Life was so different at home. Things that seemed such a big deal in Toronto didn't even register here. I enjoyed doing little things like mowing the lawn. People often stopped by to visit; it was no big deal arranging dates and times. I knew everyone, and they knew me.

My cousin drove past one day as I was mowing the lawn. "Hey," he said. "Are you interested in a job working for a development program?"

"Sure," I replied.

"Sounds good," he said. "Send over your resume." The next week I started a new job.

The office was located downtown; I worked alone. There was an occasional board meeting, but I usually scheduled my own hours. A couple of other native organizations had offices in the building, and I would often drop in to chat. I was twenty-nine years old and finally had my life on track. It would soon be time to get my own apartment. My sister mentioned that my parents were missing their privacy and were now getting a little annoyed by my schedule. I still went out a lot, especially on weekends, and bars were open until 4:00 a.m. I often arrived home on the weekends at 4:30 or 5:00 a.m. This wasn't working for my aging parents any longer; change was needed.

I gave some thought to where I might want to live, but options were limited. I didn't own a car. Plus some of the apartments I was familiar with downtown didn't really appeal to me. I wanted some place quiet. It was my thought that if all went well and I focused my search, I could possibly move into my own apartment sometime early in the New Year. It was December 1993. Then I met the man I would marry that first week in December.

I was out with friends the night before we met; I arrived in the office around 10:00 a.m. The ladies down the hall dropped in to ask me if I was interested in meeting a good-looking Mohawk; Mark assisted their clients once a month with economic development projects. He lived in Halifax. The ladies invited him to lunch, but he was going to work through and head back to Halifax early that afternoon.

I followed them to their office, and they introduced me to Mark. They were right; he was good looking. The women quickly left for their lunch break. I usually led discussions, and this was no different. We talked about our jobs and a little bit about school. He was from Ontario and was three years younger. He had attended a university in New Brunswick. The universities we both attended happened to be football rivals; he had been a tight end. I knew a little about football, so we eased into talking about the school rivalry. I was getting hungry and asked if he wanted to go out for some lunch. "Sure," he said.

We were comfortable with each other right from the start. We had an enjoyable lunch, and I invited him to contact me when he returned the next time for his scheduled visit. It was a month before I saw him next. He went home to Ontario for the holidays, and I had traveled to visit friends. We went out on our first date in January and married nine months later. I moved to Halifax full time in June, and we got our own apartment. We married in October. My family loved him from the start.

Not long after our wedding, my mother was diagnosed with breast cancer. She had a lumpectomy and went through radiation treatment. She made a full recovery but had some long-term effects to her eyes from the radiation treatment. She required drops for dry eyes and would often need more aggressive treatment due to infections caused by extreme dryness. She also had problems with dry mouth.

My husband and I moved to London, Ontario, the following year. He accepted a management position in banking, and we looked forward to the move. I worked at a nearby First Nation. It was not long after our move that I received a call from my mother saying that my father had lost his hearing and was completely deaf. My father's hearing loss was quick. It was difficult for him to deal with, and he was suffering from depression. He was sent to see specialist in Halifax, but the diagnosis was grim. The hearing loss was permanent. He was sixty-three years old.

The family was at a loss at what to do; it was so unexpected. My father started to lose weight, and his moods were unpredictable. It was by chance that he met a young man who changed his life.

I'm not certain of the events that led to my parents meeting this young man, but somehow they connected, and he stopped by the house to share his story; he too was deaf. My mother wrote notes for my father as he spoke. The young man had said he had a successful cochlear implant. He had been permanently deaf and underwent experimental treatment in London, Ontario, that restored his ability to hear. He thought our family should check out the procedure for my father; maybe he too was a candidate for treatment! My father was hopeful for the first time in months.

My family immediately went into research mode to have my father tested to see if he qualified for the treatment. A cochlear implant is a small, complex electronic device that can help provide a sense of sound to a person who is profoundly deaf or severely hard of hearing. An implant does not restore normal hearing. Instead, it can give a deaf person a useful representation of sounds in the environment and help him or her understand speech. Hearing through a cochlear implant is different from normal hearing and takes time to learn or relearn. The literature on treatment was encouraging.

The first audiologist my father visited for a recommendation refused to refer my father for treatment; his comment was that my father was too old to benefit from the implant. My family persisted. They traveled to Halifax to meet with another audiologist to review my father's case. This audiologist offered to recommend my father for treatment but doubted that the procedure would be covered by the Provincial Medical Care Insurer. It was not. The provincial insurer required more information on the procedure, and my father would need to meet with the cochlear implant team in London, Ontario, and return with a referral and treatment plan.

It was now a little over a year since my father had gone deaf. He was still dealing with bouts of depression. It was fortuitous that our recent move to London meant my parents would not need to spend additional financial resources on hotels. My parents spent a week in London; throughout that time my father was scheduled for a battery of tests that assisted the cochlear implant team in determining his suitability for the implant. At the final meeting, we were given the positive news. The team was going to recommend my father for the procedure; they were very optimistic in their belief that he would benefit from the implant. My parents returned home with the wonderful news.

It took another few months before all the details were worked out for the cochlear implant procedure. The Provincial Insurer wavered on their decision to pay for the implant and requested additional support from other specialist. It was frustrating for my father to wait; he continued to lose weight and would still have severe bouts with depression. Finally everything was approved, and the surgical procedure was scheduled. My parents would need to spend two months in London. This marked the longest period my parents were away from the community and the family. They arrived in the spring.

The surgery was a success, and my father recovered without any problems. The implant could not be tested until he completely healed. This would take six weeks. My father was nervous on the day we returned to the hospital to test the device. It was not simply turning the device on. He was required to go through a series of vocal tests that were then input into a computer. This took most of the morning. The doctor arrived, and he underwent another examination. Finally, it was time.

The device was turned on; my father heard immediately. He started to pound his hands on the armrests on the chair; his excitement could not be contained. It was the happiest I had ever seen him!

We couldn't leave right away and waited in the cafeteria while my father adjusted to the device. The noise was a little too much for him, and the volume had to be adjusted. When we arrived back to my place, my father flushed the toilet over and over. He loved the sound. We called the family with the news, and they all eagerly anticipated their return. A week later my father was allowed to go home. By this time they were both desperately homesick.

We stayed in London another couple of years and then moved to Toronto. At this time, I worked as a national coordinator for a not-for-profit. It was my first management role, and I desperately wanted to impress.

My first business dinner with my boss was going well. We were in Vancouver to meet with the regional management team. A gentleman who was a director of a major funder for our organization stopped by our table, and my boss introduced me. I was reviewing the menu and tried my best not to appear nervous. I was asked a question by the gentleman about a project I was overseeing and was in the process of answering when he casually said to me, "You know your menu's on fire!" I freaked out; it was one of those long menus, and it got caught in the candle. I was mortified, but it was an unforgettable moment!

It seemed I was prone to crazy things that seemingly happened out of the blue. I attended a conference in Ottawa and accidently dropped my car keys as I entered the elevator; they somehow fell through a crack and landed at the bottom of the elevator shaft. It took two days to retrieve them; the elevator shaft is off limits and could only be accessed by a certified elevator repairman. Another time I was heading away on business and arrived at the airport and jumped out to get my luggage; I left the car running and accidently locked the doors. I was traveling with my boss, who was already in the airport and waiting for me at the gate. It took over an hour for my roadside assistance technician to arrive and unlock the car. Our flights had to be changed for later that evening, and his luggage was pulled off the flight.

These incidences seemed to occur on a regular basis. I always had a story to tell. It certainly kept my family entertained. I loved making people laugh; it seemed in recounting my most embarrassing moments, I was able to finally share a little bit of myself that didn't hurt so much.

We lived in Toronto for a year, and I got my feet wet in understanding management principles and project coordination. I realized I enjoyed research and could easily engage with other departments and the projects they championed. People often came to me for advice, and I was selected to lead a couple of major events for the organization. It was after one of these major events that another milestone was etched in my life path.

I had been away for over a week tending to the organization's twenty-fifth anniversary celebrations in Saskatchewan. Our organization was international in scope; however, we had a national Aboriginal development program that was celebrating twenty-five years of service in Canada. The three-day celebrations went off without a hitch, and I returned home to Toronto. Exhausted, I planned to take one day off then get back to the office to oversee projects I was responsible for managing. The phone rang at around 4:00 a.m. It was my mother. My father had died; he had a major heart attack.

I was shaken but not completely surprised. My father's health had been deteriorating over the past few months, and he had already been through one close call in which his prognosis was critical. My father had diabetes, and he had been experiencing organ deterioration over the past few years. His eyesight was failing, he was deaf, and he had a strange addiction to acetaminophen. He would often go through several bottles a week, usually containing one hundred pills each. I didn't know the extent of his addiction until after his near death a few months earlier.

The doctors couldn't figure out what was ailing my father. He was experiencing serious organ failure, and various treatments they were applying didn't seem to work. They met with my mother again to review my father's medical history. It just wasn't making sense to them; he should be getting better. Usually it was a simple case of adjusting his insulin and spending a few days in the hospital to recover. But this time he was near death. The doctors probed further, "Is he taking anything?" My mother indicated it was all in his chart. The only thing she could add was the acetaminophen. They asked, "How many?" She wasn't completely sure how many he took in a day, but she knew it was a lot. This was news!

The doctors immediately changed my father's course of treatment to adjust for the amount of acetaminophen in his system; it was having a dire effect on his health. He recovered but remained in the hospital for a couple weeks. His acetaminophen addiction did not end; as soon as he was able, he returned to taking his daily doses of the over-the-counter pain pills. My father was sixty-seven years old when he died from heart failure.

His life was not an easy one. My father grew up in extreme poverty on the reserve in which he spent his entire life. His home was nothing more than a shanty. It would barely be considered habitable by today's standards, if not outright condemned. His mother died when he was a young boy, and he helped his father raise his four younger siblings. His father eventually remarried, and his stepmother bore an additional four siblings.

My father contracted tuberculosis when he was a teenager and spent three years in a rehabilitation center ten miles from the reserve. He had a big scar on one side of his back where his lung had been partially removed. He married my mother when he was around twenty-one. They had grown up together, though my mother's upbringing was considerably more fortunate. My parents had children in quick succession; by the time he was in his early thirties, he had nine children. Although my father would become an alcoholic, he didn't start drinking until his mid-thirties.

He picked up barbering while hospitalized in the tuberculosis rehabilitation center. He also became an orderly, helping out the staff as much as he could. When he was released from the hospital, it wasn't unusual for the coroner at the local hospital to call upon my father to assist in post-mortem preparations for community members who had recently passed. He often worked three jobs to meet the needs of the family and to put food on the table. Social welfare had not yet been introduced to our communities; it was imperative to work to survive. We went through many long periods when transportation was not available, and my father would often walk to and from work. One night he almost froze walking home in a snowstorm. It was a very dramatic scene when he finally burst through the door. At that time his only protection against the extreme weather was galoshes and a lightweight overcoat; they didn't provide much warmth.

He was a good man. He was good to our family, to his brothers and sisters, and helped everyone in the community in any way he could. This is the way his friends remember him, and this is the way I choose to remember him now. I remember his laughter and his wild stories of when he was young and all the dramas that played out in his life. His friends and relatives traveled from all over Nova Scotia to pay their respects to him. He made an impact on those who sought treatment at the Native Detox Center where he worked for ten years and the many people who sought him out as a barber for over thirty years. My father was just one soul trying to figure out his way, and he had a lot to learn in this lifetime!

Chapter 12

The number nine seems to play into many aspects of my life. It often appears to represent a conclusion. Even though it has played out numerous times in my adulthood, I mostly remained unaware of its influences until recently. My husband and I started reviewing events in our life and realized that nine factored in most times. Whether it was nine days, nine weeks, nine months, or nine years, it repeated itself continually. We actually did this for two days, texting each other whenever we put together another nine association. We were amazed.

Most recently when I had finished a contract, we decided we could finally afford to book a family vacation. My friend and her two children would join us as well. Both our families had struggled financially over the past three years, so it was a relief to finally put aside our strict budgets and book a holiday. As I studied the itinerary, I noted that our holiday was booked exactly nine months after I had decided to make significant changes in my life; that was in August 2013. A part of this change included eliminating alcohol from my life.

I had stopped drinking before when I went through the healing process and didn't drink for another fifteen months. However, I felt I had sacrificed enough; it was okay to drink again. We had survived the worst.

I told myself it was okay because I drank only the lightest beer available, and I hardly ever went overboard. However, I quickly relied on beer in situations of stress. I was not in a good place mentally, and the beer helped me forget that my life was in such turmoil. I would note the number of beer cans each week. Should I be concerned? Was it too many?

After a year, I knew it wasn't good. I needed to change.

I hadn't worked in three years and felt like I was at the end of my rope. In those three years, I had finished school, but I should have had a job by now. My husband was trying to be supportive, but it bothered him that I was still not working. He knew I had a range of skills and knowledge that were transferrable to many positions that were available.

However, I was still caught up in the anger and resentment of the healing process—the process I felt I was forced to endure. I hated my new house; it represented the fear that the healer exploited. I hated being in a community I didn't have any connection to; they were not of my nation. But what I hated most was the feeling that I didn't have a choice of where we lived, and we were stuck here because we couldn't afford to move.

I had never stopped reading, but by May of 2013 the reading shifted. The urgency was greater. I was reading book after book, honing my knowledge on all matters spiritual. I started making poster boards detailing spiritual concepts. I was learning at a rate that most people would have difficulty keeping up with. The concepts were easy for me to understand; I easily recognized how they related to my life and those around me. I was beginning to ease up on myself. I was being shown a way out!

Then in August, I picked up a book by James Van Praagh titled *Unfinished Business: What the Dead Can Teach Us about Life*. On the day I finished reading the book, I closed it and made the decision to quit drinking right then and there.

I was well aware of our familial addiction challenges and group tendencies. That day I made the choice to live my life in another way—one where I didn't need to count the beer cans to determine if my drinking was out of control. I was committed to move toward a life based on self-love and the knowledge that my sacrifice to quit drinking was a necessary part of my spiritual growth.

I continued to read but at the same time taught myself a little about numerology and studied the tarot. They both involved detailed study; I now feel that I have a deeper appreciation of our life lessons and the many tools we have available to help us along our journey.

I studied the tarot exactly as it was presented. I didn't skip ahead and do readings immediately. I studied each card as it was intended and learned all seventy-eight cards in the deck, both their meaning and their application. I studied like it was going to be presented in an examination. I felt it was important to eliminate any fear associated with the tarot. When I finished studying each card of the tarot, I came to the realization that my life experience had touched on each and every one of the twenty-two major arcana and the fifty-six minor ones.

In my life, and as in the deck, I had come to the end ... I had come full circle.

It was only after this study that I dared do a reading on myself. It was simple and telling. I saw clearly what the cards indicated. I would only use the cards a few more times. I knew the cards were a gift to understand my life's challenges, and every scenario that presented itself was a valuable lesson from which experience and wisdom was attained. I felt strongly that I needed to develop my own intuitive gifts without relying on the tarot to guide me.

Numerology, on the other hand, remains a constant friend. I practice by doing pyramids on random birth dates and usually carry a book with me for reference. I enjoy reviewing the lives of famous people who have crossed over and chart their lives according to their birth date pyramid. Also, if time allows, I will chart their names, especially those who had legally changed their names from their names at birth or changed their name to that of a partner. It's a satisfying hobby that I can do anywhere and is a constant reminder to myself to be mindful in all that I do.

At this time, I was moved to figure out the license plate BEVJ 368. It stayed in my mind over the three years since I had seen it and knew it was a message. I researched all meaning of the first three letters that formed the name BEV; this would lead to a website on biblical names. The name BEV was broken down in this way: Gracious Oath of God—*Peace and Harmony*; Promise—*Enlightenment*. Another interpretation is Hebrew—*Light Bringer, Radiating God's Light*.

I interpreted the meaning of the J to represent *Jesus*.

The letters BEVJ in numerology break down to the number 3. The number 3 is interpreted different ways in numerology depending on the author. It could represent the ascended masters, such as Christ Jesus, or that of the Holy Trinity *Father, Son, and the Holy Spirit*, or a triangle representing our connection between the mind, body, and spirit.

The numbers 368 add up to 8. In numerology, the number 8 is both my ruling number and my complete name number; I was born the eighth child. Finally, the number 6 represents my soul urge number derived from my name, *Paula*.

Yes, this could all be a coincidence, but I choose to see it as a message from my angels that they are watching over me and their messages will appear as they are needed.

As soon as I started to make changes in my life, my connection to intuitive messages began to expand. Before I intuitively knew I should go someplace or see someone, but I didn't hear or sense the guidance as I do now.

For example, last summer I had a dream of a young boy in the river. He had drowned. I could see him in the water; the river was flooded over its banks. I woke up feeling a little upset. Later that day, I was home relaxing and for no reason said to the kids, "Let's go to the park!" We packed up immediately, and we were at the park in about twenty minutes. I don't usually engage with people at the park and sit quietly reading while the kids play. But on this day, as I walked toward the play area near the river, I started waving my hands and calling out to a woman who was there with her young son. He was about four. The lady came over to me thinking we knew each other, but I said to her, "I just wanted to say hello."

We chatted anyway. Her son didn't have kids to play with near his home, and he was happy my sons had arrived. As we talked, the conversation got personal very quickly. The lady was very lonely. Her husband worked night shifts, and he often had to sleep during the day. Raising her young son fell on her, and she was often tired. She mentioned that she had severe kidney issues and was overcome with fear that she was going to need a kidney transplant in the next while; the doctor had recently informed her that her kidneys were operating at 20 percent. What would happen to her son if something went wrong with her!

For a moment I didn't say anything. I just let her get it all out. "You know," I said, "my mother is seventy-eight years old, and she has been functioning with 20 percent of her kidneys most of her life. She was born with a defect that she didn't even know about until well into her sixties. She follows a renal diet and lives her life pretty much normal in that regard. But up until she found out about the lack of kidney function, she ate whatever she felt like eating."

The woman was excited. "You mean she doesn't have any serious issues!"

"No, other than the odd infection, her health was never directly impacted by her lack of kidney function."

She thanked me for sharing my mother's story with her. She smiled and got up to leave; her husband would be awake soon.

The new, expanded guidance was more engaging. I was expecting that I would return to work soon, but I didn't know in what capacity. I kept going back to an advertisement for a "Request for Proposals" that I had seen on a Native Newswire. I just couldn't get it out of my head. I read it again. It seemed complicated. I didn't know if I could carry it myself, and it had a tight deadline. It was directed to "agencies" and "businesses." Finally I thought I would go for it.

I started on the Response for Proposal or RFP. It was a detailed proposal and required a significant amount of work to satisfy the deliverable schedule. I researched for three days and then began my RFP. It wasn't long before I felt overwhelmed. There was no way I could do all this work. I thought to myself, *I'm not even that knowledgeable in this field of study!* I stopped writing. *Maybe not*, I thought.

I decided to meditate. I realized that my fear was my only obstacle and that I needed to get past it. As I went into meditation, the sensations began, and so did the messages. Ideas were being given to me. I asked questions and received the answers. Even the budget amount was provided. I went back to the RFP and started again. I researched the new ideas and realized that with some work, they could be easily integrated into the RFP. They were new so I had to make it up as I went along. I also needed to itemize the budget in such a manner that would ensure the amount that was given to me in meditation was attained.

I was not surprised to win the RFP selection; I was amazed!

Chapter 13

My husband and I were working on the house. I received a text from the healer to ask if I had talked to my husband yet about the additional release sessions. The healer was still insisting that my husband needed them and that he was still thinking of cheating on me. He said Mark would not be allowed to move into the new house if his mind was not right. He again said, "They will stop him!" I was scheduled to continue with my mediation sessions.

I called my husband outside to talk because we were told never to discuss any concerns in the house since it would weaken the protection medicine. If we did, we had to smudge right away.

By this time I had already read quite a number of spiritual-related books that gave me some confidence that evil didn't exist around every corner. Growing up Catholic, it was easier for the healer to manipulate me because I grew up with the constant thought of eternal damnation and a fiery hell. His assertions that we would be punished for every sin and providing the detailed description of that punishment didn't exactly help in assuaging my deep-rooted fears of the devil, hell, and damnation.

My husband, however, didn't have such fears. He didn't attend church as a child and wasn't influenced one way or the other. However, his shame and guilt lay in his lack of connection to his nation and the cultural traditions associated with his clan. Although my husband studied business in university, he also completed courses on indigenous studies and was well informed on his nation's history. Unfortunately, there was no interaction with the traditional peoples of his nation who maintained the cultural heritage and traditions. His mother's family discouraged learning the traditional ways and were part of the Anglican Church. Although his mother was Native, his father is Dutch. This too seemed to create self-imposed barriers to connecting in any meaningful way with the traditional community. He was ashamed of his Dutch lineage.

I was ready to talk. I'd had enough. I told Mark that I wasn't planning on returning to the healer; I was ending the healing process that day. I reviewed all the healer had said to me in our sessions regarding my husband's intentions to cheat and that if he didn't do release work, the guides would not allow him to move into the house. He was shocked. Everything came pouring out: the manipulation, the threats, the fear, the coercion, and the betrayal. I couldn't handle it anymore.

My husband sent the healer a simple text indicating that we were done, but the healer replied to my cell phone: "You are so close to finishing. Why stop now?" I didn't reply; there was no need.

Fortunately, I had started school in September, and we were busy working on the house. We also had our boys to look after and ensure all of their needs were being met. I didn't have time to think of all that had happened with the healer. Every day was scheduled to maximize the number of hours we could spend on finishing the house. On the weekends, we packed lunches and stayed at the house all day. The boys spent a lot of time next door with their grandmother.

We did everything in the interior. Initially my husband was to work on the house himself, but when we started, it was just too much for one person. I had to help. I didn't mind the work; it kept me from thinking too much. We managed to move along quickly. The entire house had been insulated, dry-walled, plastered, and painted by mid-December. In addition to the labor, I managed all the selections for the flooring, cabinets, appliances, lighting, doors, knobs, and anything else that went into the home. The cistern and septic were installed, as was the furnace. The electrical and plumbing were completed in December.

Although we were directed by the healer to move into our house in December, we felt confident that one month was not going to make much of a difference. We probably could have done it if we really pushed it, but I did not want to pressure my husband. We had enough of that over the past year.

Exams for school came and went. I managed to achieve academic honors in my program. I was booked to travel home for the Christmas holidays to help relieve my siblings, who were now providing twenty-four-hour care to my ailing mother. I drove two days each way and brought the kids with me. It was an intense week with my mother. Her needs were very extensive. I was appreciative of all the work my siblings put into her care; it was nonstop.

While I was away, my husband managed to finish the flooring throughout the house; he finished the trim soon after. The cabinets were installed, and we were ready. On January 27 we moved into our new home. We had completed our task.

I graduated from my program with honors in May 2012; I no longer felt like an academic failure. But all of these achievements could not hold back my self-loathing.

I would not accept the house as my own. I felt like a stranger in a strange land. I felt trapped. The house was beautiful, but it represented something I didn't want to remember. My thoughts were constantly focused on getting a job so I could get away from the community. It seemed every attempt to find a job was blocked. I had never experienced this before. I was always able to find something, meet somebody, or get some recommendation. Not this time.

Every day was another day I didn't have a job. My anxiety was increasing, and so was my resentment. I would sit outside and have a beer and look at everything with such disdain. I absolutely hated it! A few times I thought of moving home to Cape Breton. I tried to convince my husband that the move would be great. The kids could spend a lot more time with all their cousins, I implored! He didn't want to leave his job.

The only person who knew about my hatred of the house was my husband. However, he was also dealing with his own family issues. This seemed to irritate us even more, and the resentment grew deeper. Fortunately, we were never down at the same time, and we didn't make any rash decisions. When he was feeling low, I would help him manage, and when I was feeling low, he would do the same. This was how our relationship survived. We knew how to balance each other.

When I look back on that time, it was similar to what may be classified as post-traumatic stress syndrome. I managed to survive the event, but I was just holding on. With the boys being out of school that first summer, at least my focus was on their care, and I managed to set aside my anxieties. But as soon as they returned to school, the feelings returned. My husband was trying to give me space to heal, but he wanted me to work too. It was a never-ending circle. I wanted to move, but I needed a job to move. I couldn't find a job, and we were still there!

This went on into the following summer, when I finally decided I was going to change my life. I knew the change needed to come from within. No one could help me with this step. I had to do it myself.

Once the change started, it just kept rolling. My husband was still pressuring me to get a job, but I didn't worry about it as much anymore. I knew good things were coming, but it would be in divine right time. I was becoming stronger; my faith was moving me forward. My energy shifted, and people noticed the lightness around me; I appeared more youthful. I was constantly given healing strength by the energies that surrounded me.

I now danced around my home, full of joy and gratitude to be provided with such a beautiful shelter!

Chapter 14

The release sessions continued to chronicle my life. Events were intertwined as I reached my thirties and forties. My life was more settled. There was not the angst of my childhood, teen years, and young adult years. I didn't leave as much debris as I worked my way through life. However, I was still guilt ridden about all those I had hurt and unsettled in that I would be found out!

The year after my father died, my husband and I moved to a smaller town an hour from Toronto. I had accepted an office manager position at another organization that was located back in London, Ontario. My husband accepted a consultant position near where we live today. We chose to live in a small community located halfway between our jobs. Fortunately for my husband, he was able to work from home most days.

Our lives were busy. We traveled a lot for both pleasure and business. We thought about having children, but I knew for quite some time that I would face challenges with conceiving a child. I had an ectopic pregnancy, and the prognosis was not very good. We were content with our lives. We celebrated in the new millennium quietly with my mother-in-law.

My mother would visit on occasion, and we would travel around southern Ontario visiting her sisters, nieces, and nephews. It was always a good time. I enjoyed all the stories from their childhood and of the people who lived on our reserve when they were growing up. It was wonderful to hear my mother speak with her sisters in our beautiful Mi'kmaq language.

In 2001 I had turned thirty-seven. I was shaken by the events of September 11 and the attacks on the World Trade Center and the Pentagon. It was so senseless. My view on life and children changed.

By this time, I was fairly certain I wouldn't have children. My husband and I didn't use contraception for a long time, so we knew intervention would be necessary. We were fine with remaining childless, though I thought my husband would make a wonderful father. He had a wonderful way with children; they adored him.

My sister had a baby in August of that year, and I went to visit her soon after the events of September 11. The first moment I held my nephew in my arms, I fell in love. I knew then that I would do whatever it would take to have a baby.

When I returned home, I started my research. I didn't want to go the usual route of referrals through my family doctor to a fertility specialist. I was getting older and felt I needed to look after this right away. I e-mailed a fertility doctor at a highly respected clinic in Ottawa. I didn't really expect to hear back since I didn't have a referral. I gave him a little information about my case and noted my worry due to my age.

In a couple days, his assistant sent me an e-mail asking for more information. I sent the information the doctor required immediately. She called to notify me that the doctor had agreed to see me, but they were not booking any appointments until the

New Year; they would let me know in a few months when an appointment became available.

My husband and I went away on vacation in February of the following year. I was still waiting to hear from the clinic. I was lying on the beach when my cell phone rang. It was the doctor's assistant; they had an appointment for the following month. From here everything moved quickly. Tests were completed, assessments were done, and decisions were made. We were going to start in vitro fertilization in June of that same year.

I love to mountain bike and would often go out for long jaunts through the TransCanada bike trails that run through our area. I cycled hard; I had a lot on my mind. Was I doing the right thing in moving forward with IVF! Would it work! I prayed to God to give me some sign, any sign, to let me know I was on the right path.

I was breathing hard, moving faster. I knew there was a bend in the path and I needed to be careful of other traffic that was coming from the opposite direction. It was a blind spot that often was overlooked until it was too late. I slowed and took the corner; there on the path were two fawns. I slowly came to a stop and got off my bike. I walked toward the baby deer; I was careful as the mother could be near. They didn't move. I was close enough to touch them now. I put my hand out, and one moved toward it; the other stayed behind, too timid to move forward. It was like time stopped; I didn't want to ruin the moment, but I knew I should leave. I said good-bye to the fawns and got back on my bike. I had my sign. I wept all the way home.

I finished my contract at the end of May and chose not to extend it until the IVF treatment was finished. For the moment we would focus on the treatment procedures. The whole process worked wonderfully. My pregnancy was confirmed in August, and we knew immediately, through an ultrasound that I was pregnant with twins.

I loved being pregnant and got very big. My sister said I looked like Humpty Dumpty. I carried to full term, and the boys were born in February 2003. They were named Nathaniel and Bradley. We celebrated their baptismal with my family in Cape Breton. I stayed home with the boys for the next two and a half years.

I finally went back to work when a friend asked if I would help him open a store. My husband and I had flexible hours, so we continued to care for the boys ourselves. I didn't know much about the retail business, but I quickly learned. I opened the store in six weeks. I was busy with the store and looking after the boys. My mother-in-law helped us out as well. We made plans to go home to Cape Breton for a family celebration that summer.

Prior to our departure home, I was having some feelings of unease. I would see flashes of light as I ran up the stairway to our bedroom. My mind was continually making plans to stay at a hotel the night of the wedding anniversary celebration, but we were scheduled to stay at my mother's. The night of the celebration, I went out with my sisters; my husband stayed with the boys. I arrived home late and couldn't get into the house. My husband opened the door and went back to bed.

I was eating pizza in the kitchen, and my mother came in and we started arguing. She was sure I was too drunk to open the door; she had left the key in the mailbox after all. I said it didn't work; I still couldn't open the door. I insisted the door handle was locked. The key was only for the deadbolt. It went on, and the fight escalated very quickly. My years of pent-up anger at my mother came pouring out; there was no going back.

My husband and sister came downstairs to intervene, but it was already too late. The situation was out of control; I was out of control. I left that night and went to my brother's house. I didn't see my mother again for two years.

I was in the store. We had since moved to a new location, which was situated on the owner's property. There was a small apartment above the store that the owner stayed when he was in town. It was Sunday, and the earlier rush had already dispersed. I heard banging coming from the apartment. At first I thought an animal somehow got in and went to check. There was nothing there. The banging continued. I called my husband to come have a look. I was getting nervous. He would be about a half hour.

As I waited, I stood outside. I was feeling unnerved. A neighbor who lived across the street came by, and I told him what had happened. He went upstairs to have a look around. There was nothing, he said. Then he heard the sounds too. He looked again. He said he would go speak to an elder in the community. My husband finally came by as well. He heard the bangs but couldn't find anything either. The neighbor returned. The elder said there was a matter that I needed to look after.

I closed the store and went home. The following day, I got a call at work from my sister-in-law. She said my mother was in the hospital and she had necrotizing fasciitis—flesh-eating disease. I had to call my brother right away.

My brother answered his phone on the first ring. "Paula, you need to come home immediately. The doctors are taking Mom into surgery in a few minutes to amputate her arm. They don't think she will make it through the night."

I was in a daze. My husband made arrangements for me to fly out on the next available flight. When I arrived at the hospital, my mother was in the intensive care unit. Her arm had been amputated to the shoulder, and she had some bacteria spread to her chest. They could not put her on penicillin; she was allergic. It would need to be high doses of other types of antibiotics. She was in a drug-induced coma.

It was a few days before Easter. Her situation was assessed on an hour-to-hour basis. She had made it through the night; the doctors were surprised. Relatives, friends, and community members brought food to the hospital for the family. The first couple of days we were there around the clock. Her condition remained the same. We began taking shifts. I did the overnight shift. A couple of my nephews and a young man who was close to my mother kept me company.

It was Good Friday, and I was settling in for my overnight shift. Most of the family who were there during the day had already left. My nephew and I were sitting in one of the family suites. My cousin walked in, and she had a cross that was very old. It was only taken out of the box on Good Friday. The wooden cross would be taken to those who needed healing. It was nearly reaching the time that the cross would be put away for another year. She had to rush in from another community located twenty-five kilometers away.

Someone within the family would need to pray for my mother; I was the only one. My nephew didn't feel comfortable with prayer. She asked me if I believed in God. If I didn't then someone else would need to do the pray. I timidly said, "Yes, I believe in God."

We said a prayer, and I held the cross in my hands. It was quite big, one that would have hung on a wall. I start to pray for my mother and her healing. As I did this, I sensed white light pulsating through my body. My eyes closed, and everything started flashing white. It was like it was spinning throughout my body. I began to shake. After a couple of minutes, I gave the cross to my cousin. I was deeply affected. I hugged my cousin and began to cry; it was as though every emotion in me had been exposed, and I sobbed uncontrollably.

My mother was brought out of her coma a couple of days later. She was beginning to stabilize. In her confusion it took a while for everything to fully register; my sister had to explain a few times what had happened to her. I returned home to Ontario; it had been a week since my mother's surgery.

I was home for a couple of days when I noticed spots on my body. Soon after, I broke out into a painful, blistering rash that lasted nearly a month. This had never happened to me before.

The following month, I decided to return to Cape Breton but this time with my family. I had planned to spend a month helping out with my mother's care at the hospital. My husband stayed two weeks. It was a time of reconciliation. My mother and I talked for a long time. We both regretted what had happened, and I apologized for my actions that led to our estrangement. Our healing was a slow process; we both needed to trust again.

She spent six weeks in the hospital and an additional two months in a rehabilitation center. When she arrived home, she needed assistance for the first couple months; however, it wasn't long before she was again living on her own. My mother's faith in God did not waver; it sustained her throughout her painful recovery. The source of the necrotizing fasciitis was never determined.

The boys are now getting older. They are four years old and starting junior kindergarten. It's their second year of school. I closed my friend's store following my mother's surgery. I was no longer interested in managing the business. It was time to move on.

I went back to contract work, doing small projects for various Aboriginal organizations. The projects were a lot more stimulating than managing the store, and I was again utilizing my research skills. I completed several small contracts for an organization in which I would later accept a longer-term contract. I was drawn to promotional work but didn't enjoy the spotlight. I felt more secure behind the scenes, executing every detail and coordinating the activities. I was able to come up with ideas quickly and knew exactly how to position them.

At one time I participated in a career assessment to determine a line of work that would best match my skills and interests. I was asked to answer all questions truthfully and to the best of my knowledge. The assessment took the whole morning and included various components. I tested well on the knowledge-based component, but there seemed to be some difficulty in assessing my interests. When it came time to provide final results for a possible career match, nothing registered. The instructor thought it was a mistake; that had never happened before. There were on average three to four career matches provided to each candidate. He ran the test again; still nothing. I had hoped the assessment would finally provide me with some insight into possible career options I could seriously consider for the future. I was disappointed.

I later joked about the assessment. "I guess it means I'm meant to make it up as I move along. No shortcuts here!"

Work that others found tedious didn't bother me; I loved bringing ideas to life. My focus was sharp, and I honed my skills. I enjoyed working alone and didn't mind the long hours involved in projects that required in-depth research. I often attended conferences promoting one project or another. It was at one of these conferences that I received a call from my sister. My mother was in the hospital; she had fallen and broken her femur.

Apparently my mother lost her balance and fell on the side on which her arm had been amputated. There was nothing to break her fall. She was not wearing her medical alert necklace; it had been irritating her neck, and she had taken it off a little earlier. It was on a table across the room. My mother knew she had to get to the necklace. The pain was excruciating, but she knew she had to drag herself across the room. She passed out a couple times from the pain. When she recounted the story, she said she now knew what injured war veterans went through to get themselves through a battlefield.

She slowly moved herself inch by inch across the living room floor. It took her over an hour to reach the other side of the room. When she got to the table, she had to turn herself to be able to reach up and grab the tablecloth that was hanging down. Once she did this, she was able to pull on it, and the necklace dropped to the floor. She notified the medical alert administers, who in turn called an ambulance. They also attempted to call the emergency contacts that included two of my sisters and a brother. They were all away at meetings. The ambulance crew couldn't get in the house; the doors were locked. They could see my mother on the floor; they tried all the windows and doors. A neighbor came by and was going to break down the door, but then he ran over to another sister's home to let her know what was happening. She had the key; she made her way over to the house, terrified she would find Mom dead. It was all very dramatic!

The pain was excruciating for my mother. The paramedics had to provide her with morphine to move her onto the stretcher. There was another hospital stay, and once again my mother entered the rehabilitation center. She fought through the therapy until she was able to walk again. She used a cane for a while but soon didn't need that either. She was seventy-five at this time and enjoyed her independence.

In 2010 I started on a full-time contract. I loved the work promoting a new program. I felt confident in my work and truly enjoyed engaging with all the staff. I thought this could be it. Maybe this time I had fallen into a field of work in which I would eventually settle. I worked hard, diligently. For ten months everything was wonderful. Then I met the healer.

Chapter 15

My life had taken a precarious path. I believe on a couple occasions, I had one foot over the cliff, and one more step or misstep would have resulted in grievous injury or even death. I am thankful each and every day that I was shown a way out—that I was guided out of the darkness!

I'm sure for some this seems a bit of an exaggeration, but I knew the darkness that had taken up residence in the heart. I knew the guilt and shame intimately because we had shared many moments reliving and chastising ourselves for all the pain and suffering we had caused. We were merciless in our attempts to punish ourselves—to never forget one single act of evil we inflicted on others. We examined ourselves under the brightest light so all flaws were exposed!

This darkness primed me; I was a walking billboard with fear, guilt, and shame written all over it in gigantic neon letters. I made myself an easy target.

Then I came to love myself—not in a conceited way but a knowing that I am part of God. I wouldn't knowingly hurt God, so why would I hurt myself!

Today I am proud to be a new walking billboard—a billboard that flashes big letters that are bathed in white light and radiate love, forgiveness, and healing. This light connects me to all the universal energies that aid and support me. My connection to my mother remains strong.

Three years earlier, my mother had fallen for a second time, which resulted in a broken hip; she would not fully recover from this fall. Her health was starting to deteriorate, and her bones took longer to heal due to osteoporosis. During these three years, her every medical need was met, and any construction on the home that was required to accommodate her declining mobility was made. My siblings reorganized their lives to ensure my mother had twenty-four-hour care. They were there for every doctor's consultation, appointment, or hospitalization. Her every need was met.

I went home to visit my mother a couple months before she passed away. Every part of her body was pained at the slightest touch. She was completely bedridden. Sleep was intermittent.

I spent a week with my mom; in this time she would occasional give me a smile, a little laugh, or a gentle look. They passed quickly; the pain was too intense.

Back home in Ontario, I woke from a dream feeling a little bit uncertain of its meaning. It was my mother; she had walked down the stairs and was standing near me in a housecoat. She seemed a little bewildered. She appeared as she would have been in her late forties or early fifties. I asked her how she got down the stairs, but she just stared at me. The dream ended before she could reply.

I called her that day, but she could only say a few words before she was overcome by pain. A week later she was admitted into the palliative unit. She was aware of her surroundings until she was taken to her room, and then she became unconscious. Friends and relatives streamed in to pay their respects; her room was never empty. She didn't regain consciousness and died three days later. As we said our good-byes, flashes danced around the ceiling in her room. "Do you see them!" I kept asking. No one else did.

Mom was brought home one last time for her wake. Our family gathered around her—not in grief but admiration and respect. We knew she was with her loved ones—with my father. Her heaven's wait was over. The love she shared would remain her legacy, as would her final teachings to her family—teachings that in experiencing her last earthly lessons would help teach us patience, compassion for the elderly, and unconditional love.

These teachings, shared in her greatest time of need, brought with them grace to all those who provided her love, comfort, nourishment, and prayer. Her love lives on in each of us.

When my mother passed away last September, I had just started my journey. It is now nine months later, and she is participating in my birth yet again! She helped bring me peace, and in that peace I am the light.

Afterword

The journey to healing starts in many different ways. For some unknown reason, we are plucked from our path and presented with a different course. This new direction at the moment we are shown it is neither right nor wrong! It's what's in our hearts that make it good or not so good. This holds true for spiritual healers as well.

Though my experience with an Aboriginal healer/seer was not a favorable one, my belief holds strong that Aboriginal traditional healing methods play a crucial role in supporting the healing journey of our Aboriginal peoples. However, these healing practices should not be hidden, and they should definitely not create fear!

Integrating healing methods into mainstream Aboriginal health services encourages us to take a bold step toward demystifying healing and creating transparency. This is especially important for the development of young or novice healing apprentices who are new to their spiritual gifs and need to seek mentorship from more experienced healers.

I knew the healer as an acquaintance a year before this happened; he was somewhat aware of our lives through a couple of sources. That is why I took the messages to heart; I thought he could be trusted.

Exactly two weeks after I received guidance to write this book, I signed a publishing agreement with Balboa Press, a division of Hay House, Inc., to self-publish my book.

After I signed the agreement and returned it via electronic signature, I decided to relax for a few moments. Seated at the table where I had been writing, I closed my eyes. I automatically fell into a meditative state. The energies quickly surrounded me. My arms were moved to relax at my sides with my palms facing up. Energy pulsated through them. It shot through my body, arching my back. I began to weep; I keep repeating, *"I am in awe … I am in awe!"*

About the Author

Paula hails from a small First Nation community in Cape Breton, Nova Scotia. For those unfamiliar with the term *First Nation*, it is reserve land that has been set aside by the federal government for the exclusive use of registered Indians in Canada. Paula is Mi'kmaq; she is one of nine children.

Paula spent many years living in Toronto and other areas in southern Ontario. She is currently a consultant and certified public relations professional. Over the past fifteen years, she has completed projects in the areas of First Nation governance, health, community development, trades, and promotion. Her interest in travel inspired her to accept a position as a flight attendant in Jeddah, Saudi Arabia. In this role, she traveled through Eastern Africa, United Arab Emirates, India, and the kingdom of Saudi Arabia. While her professional passion is research, she spends much of her personal time pursuing spiritual development and numerology. Paula lives with her husband and her twin boys in southern Ontario.

CPSIA information can be obtained at www.ICGtesting.com
Printed in the USA
LVOW07s1039130814

398806LV00001B/8/P